Mark Phillip Smith

Lake Victoria
Basin Cichlids

Everything About History, Setting Up an
Aquarium, Health Concerns, and Spawning

Filled with Full-color Photographs
Illustrated by Michele Earle-Bridges

BARRON'S

CONTENTS

INTRODUCTION

The cichlids of the Lake Victoria basin comprise a unique group of cichlids found in the African continent. Of late, the scientific community has begun to give this sorely overlooked area of African ichthyofauna more careful attention. Fascinating information and plenty of new discoveries are anticipated in the near future.

The Scope of This Book

Lake Victoria basin cichlids include not only those species that inhabit Lake Victoria proper but also those that reside in surrounding lakes, swamps, and rivers. The overall reason for this grouping is that many of the cichlids from Lake Victoria and the surrounding smaller lakes, swamps, and rivers bear a remarkably close relationship to each other in overall physical and genetic parameters. Because of this, both hobbyists and ichthyologists lump nearly all of them together when discussing, maintaining, or studying them in regards to their physical appearance, coloration, common ancestry, and husbandry needs. Since many species from such surrounding lakes, swamps, and rivers are currently making their way into the hobby or have been in the hobby for a number of years side by side with Lake Victoria cichlids, including them in this book along with the cichlids of Lake Vic-

The rocky cliff in the background gives an indication of the varied topography surrounding Lake Victoria. View from Entebbe, Uganda.

toria proper seems reasonable. For ease of reference, the author will refer to Lake Victoria and the surrounding lakes, swamps, and rivers as the Lake Victoria basin.

In addition to Lake Victoria, the significant East African lakes considered part of the Lake Victoria basin are Lakes Kivu, Albert, Edward, George, and Kyoga. The names of many smaller lakes, swamps, and rivers associated with the aforementioned lakes would make too great a listing here. Those germane to the species mentioned in this book will be indicated in more detail in the species account (see pp. 56–87).

What Are Cichlids?

Cichlids are members of the order Perciformes that possess two fused lower pharyngeal bones (bones located in the throat) in the shape of a triangle. These, at a casual glance, appear to be a single bone. Depending on the teeth present on this fused bone, one can make a good guess as to what the fish in question feeds on. For example, if the teeth on the pharyngeal bone are thick with flat tops, the fish is likely to

The single continuous dorsal fin, one of several characteristics of cichlids, is clearly seen in this male **Pundamilia nyererei.**

consume hard-shelled organisms such as crustaceans or mollusks. If the teeth are very thin and elongate, then the cichlid is likely to consume small, soft-bodied organisms such as aquatic insect larvae or plankton. Although well-known for this anatomic arrangement, the family Cichlidae is not the only one to possess it. This feature is shared by wrasses of the family Labridae, the surfperches of the family Embiotocidae, and the damselfish of the family Pomacentridae. Additional features that distinguish cichlids are a single pair of nostrils, a toothless palate, an interrupted lateral line, an anal fin with three or more spines, ctenoid or cycloid

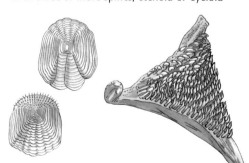

Left: Cycloid (top) and ctenoid scales. Right: Pharyngeal bone of a typical cichlid.

scales, and a single, continuous dorsal fin composed of spines and soft rays.

Cichlids are also categorized as secondary-division freshwater fish. This means that the ancestor of today's cichlids were marine fish. At some time in the past, this ancestor invaded and successfully adapted to a freshwater environment.

All cichlids are egg layers and can be placed into two general categories in regards to their methods of reproduction. One group will lay their eggs onto some sort of surface. The other group will brood their eggs in their mouth, usually performed by the female. Most mouth-brooding species will spawn on some sort of surface like the top of a rock or on the sand. In contrast, some spawn in midwater away from any kind of substrate. Postembryo parental care varies between species. Some abandon their offspring days after becoming fully formed. Others care for their young for several months and abandon them when they have reached a considerable age. As a rule, females brood the eggs to full term.

Additional anatomic structures that set cichlids apart from other kinds of fish include subdivided cheek muscles allowing exact jaw movements, a line showing the fusion point of the two halves of the lower pharyngeal bone, a long deep furrow on the lateral face of the ear bones, the opening of the intestine always lying on the left side of the stomach, and the first coil of the intestine always lying on the left side of the body. These internal features are not clearly discernible while observing a living cichlid and can be determined only by dissection.

Cichlids are found throughout many nontropical and tropical areas of the world. In the New World, they range from southern Texas southward through Central and South America to the northern regions of Argentina and southern Uruguay. They are also present on the Caribbean Islands of Cuba and Hispaniola. In the Old World, cichlids are found throughout sub-Saharan Africa, Israel, Syria, southern Iran at the Straits of Hormuz, Madagascar, southern India, and Sri Lanka. There are approximately 2,000 species, described and undescribed, with many more likely to be found in the near future. In fact, from 1997 through 1999, 60 new species were formally described.

All of the Haplochromines of the Lake Victoria basin practice mouthbrooding as their means of reproduction. Pictured is a brooding female **Pundamilia nyererei.**

Cichlids of the Lake Victoria Basin

Of the ten families of fish represented in the Lake Victoria basin, the one family that overshadows all others in terms of numbers and diversity is the family Cichlidae. In the African continent, this family is represented throughout most river systems and, particularly, in most of the great lakes of Africa. The cichlids of the Lake Victoria basin have colonized and evolved into a vast array of endemic species, making this basin one the greatest repositories of cichlid species in Africa. The cichlids constitute over 90 percent of the total number of fish species in the Lake Victoria basin. Current estimates place the number of cichlid species, including those formally described by science as well as those recognized as new and that have not been formally

described, at approximately 600. If one takes into account the number of species that existed before the deleterious effects that the human populations have had (principally upon Lake Victoria and Lake Kyoga), the total number of species was probably over 1,000.

Worldwide distribution of the family Cichlidae.

Lake
Victoria
Basin

Oreochromis variabilis *is one of only two species of Tilapiines that naturally occur in Lake Victoria.*

Both male and female Astatoreochromis allauadi *possess the same coloration. Pictured is a female from Lake Nawampasa.*

Three categories of cichlids are found in the Lake Victoria basin and are categorized based upon their ancestral relationships to each other. However, only one dominates. It contains over 99 percent of the cichlid fauna of the basin. The predominant category is referred to as the Haplochromines. These make up all of the species in the *Haplochromis* genus (and those species formerly contained in that genus) from the Lake Victoria basin. Every species in this group practices mouthbrooding for reproductive purposes.

The second category is the Tilapiines, which make up five species. Although not significant in terms of numbers of species, they are nonetheless important from a fisheries perspective. Two species naturally occur in Lake Victoria and Lake Kyoga: *Nyasalapia variabilis*, a mouthbrooder, and *Oreochromis esculentus*, a substrate spawner. The three nonnative Tilapiines, *Oreochromis niloticus, O. leucostictus*, and *Tilapia zillii*, are substrate spawners. These three nonnative cichlids, along with the native *O. esculentus*, are the only substrate-spawning cichlids residing in the Lake Victoria basin.

The last category contains a single species, *Astatoreochromis alluaudi*, which is found

throughout the Lake Victoria basin. Even though this species looks much like the Haplochromines of the basin, it has certain anatomic features that set it apart. It has a high number of anal spines, four to six versus three in the Haplochromines. It has a rounded caudal fin, which is truncated or subtruncated in the Haplochromines. *A. alluaudi* also has a higher number of egg dummies on the anal fin, up to four rows, in contrast to the fewer, smaller egg dummies in the Haplochromines. In this species, male/female coloration is nearly the same, while the males of the Haplochromines possess markedly different coloration than females.

Natural Habitats and Feeding Specializations

Up until the last couple of decades, the Haplochromines of the Lake Victoria basin were assumed to inhabit a uniform biotope, that being a sandy/muddy bottom with papyrus reeds near the shore. As more and more detailed studies of these cichlids' natural habitats came to pass, some of the lakes considered part of the Lake Victoria basin (the foremost being Lake Victoria itself) have been found to consist of a

Top: Color mutations are regularly encountered in the cichlids of the Lake Victoria basin. Pictured is a male blue mutation of **Pundamilia nyererei.**

Middle: The popular "Haplochromis" sp. Flameback is known to produce color mutations, such as this blue variant.

Bottom: Melanism is a commonly encountered color mutation in cichlids of the Lake Victoria basin. Pictured is a melanistic **Xystichromis phytophagus** *from Lake Kanyaboli, Kenya.*

wide variety of habitats much like that seen in Lake Malawi and Lake Tanganyika. The cichlids of the Lake Victoria basin have utilized every possible habitat. This includes living in the rocks, over the rocks, over sandy/muddy areas, in reed and grass beds, and even in the open waters of the lake.

The feeding specializations recognized within the Lake Victoria basin are numerous. They include piscivores, zooplanktivores, algae eaters, algae (rock) scrappers, paedophores, plant scrappers, invertebrate suckers—sucking out snail flesh from the shell, invertebrate crushers—crushing snail shells to get at the flesh, crab eaters, sponge eaters, phytoplanktivores, scale eaters, and detritivores.

Color Mutations

That many Haplochromines from the Lake Victoria basin natually produce a variety of color mutations has been known for some time. Some of the more well-known mutations that have been caught or that infrequently occur in captive, raised stocks include the following. A piebald mutation is mainly black-and-white blotched. An OB mutation is orange-and-black blotched, which, in some instances, can be nearly entirely orange with tiny black spots peppering the body. Additionally, a blue mutation, a black mutation, a yellow-to-orange mutation, and an anal fin mutation where the anal fin coloration is primarily yellow, orange, red, or black have been seen.

This undescribed Astatotilapia *species, currently going under the trade name of* Haplochromis *sp. Red Tail, was initially misidentified as* Haplochromis obliquidens. *Pictured is a male in spawning dress.*

The degree that some or all of these color mutations manifest themselves varies throughout the Lake Victoria basin. Many of these mutations have been found to occur in rock-dwelling species. Whether or not some or all of them occur in open-water species remains to be seen. In regards to a particular area of Lake Victoria that was thoroughly sampled, approximately 20 percent of the rock-dwelling species from the Mwanza Gulf were shown to produce such color mutations irregularly. According to

This melanistic Astatotilapia aeneocolor *was collected at Katwe Bay, Lake Edward.*

the latest studies conducted on these mutations from the Mwanza Gulf, they were found to occur more commonly in some groups of cichlids than in others. For instance, color mutations appeared to be more common among the snail shellers and epilithic (rock) algae scrappers while being much less common in the insectivores, planktivores, plant scrappers, and piscivores. Also, the piebald and OB mutations occur at higher densities in a given population of rock-dwelling cichlids where the transparency of the water is at its clearest, such as at islands, and less so along the shoreline where the transparency of the water is markedly worse due to shoreline sediment runoff. The only other nearby lake known to have a large percentage of color mutations among its Haplochromines is Lake Kivu.

More detailed surveys of the rest of the bodies of water within the Lake Victoria basin may show that color mutations occur more commonly than initially thought. Of the several hundred cichlids the author has collected in Lakes Edward and George, representing approximately 20 species, a single mutation was found. It was a melanistic *Astatotilapia aeneocolor*, found at Katwe Bay in northern Lake Edward.

Using the Name Haplochromis

The origin and use of the name *Haplochromis* was first used by Hilgendorf in 1888 as a sub-genus of the genus *Chromis*. The new subgenus was named *Haplochromis obliquidens*, a species endemic to Lake Victoria. In the ensuing years, various ichthyologists of the day found that correctly identifying *H. obliquidens* was nearly impossible. Apparently, it was described as different species by several scientists in the early days of Lake Victoria cichlid research. This sub-genus name was elevated by Boulenger to generic status in 1906 and later came to encompass most of the cichlids of the Lake Victoria basin. (Note that most work being performed focused on the cichlids of Lake Victoria and not so much on the other bodies of water within the Lake Victoria basin.) Other genera names were proposed. However, the genus *Haplochromis* dominated and was eventually recognized and used by ichthyologists studying the cichlids of this region of Africa. For well over 100 years, those working on the cichlids of the Lake Victoria basin realized how difficult it was to categorize the species. They frequently indicated how uncertain their understanding was of this giant species flock of cichlids.

Perhaps the most well-known ichthyologist who worked with the cichlids of the Lake Victoria basin from the 1950s through the early 1980s was Dr. Humphrey Greenwood. With the current knowledge of the day, he proposed that these cichlids were polyphyletic. In other words, they belonged to several different ancestors that invaded and populated the lake during its early history. In order to justify this view, he erected several new genera, not at the subgeneric level, but at full generic status.

Greenwood's newly erected genera began to be called into question when a newer generation of ichthyologists began to survey and collect large numbers of new species from Lake Victoria within the past 15 years. As they attempted to categorize their new finds within Greenwood's new genera, they began to see that they could not unequivocally place many of the new species they found into any of the new genera. In fact, many new species seemed to form bridges between two genera, calling into question the validity of Greenwood's definitions of his new genera. As a result, many ichthyologists abandoned Greenwood's new genera and opted to fall back upon using the old genus name of *Haplochromis* until a more precise way of defining naturally occurring groups could be ascertained.

This newer breed of ichthyologist eventually proved that the cichlids of Lake Victoria form a monophyletic group. In other words, they all descended from a single common ancestor that invaded the lake in its early history. With this more accurate assessment of Lake Victoria's cichlids, the implication is also made that the Haplochromines from the surrounding lakes, swamps, and rivers are also part of this monophyletic group. What is now seen as a more accurate way of categorizing the cichlids of the Lake Victoria basin is to focus primarily on their feeding specializations, habitat preference, and coloration. Of course, internal and external physical structures continue to play a role in this categorization process.

Neochromis nigricans *is the type species of the genus Neochromis. Pictured is a male collected from Lake Victoria at Entebbe, Uganda.*

The generic placement of many Lake Victoria basin cichlids remains unknown, such as with the Lake Victoria endemic "Haplochromis" sp. Flameback.

The introduction of the Nile perch, **Lates niloticus,** *into Lake Victoria and Lake Kyoga, has contributed to the extinction of over 200 species of cichlids.*

Currently, the foremost ichthyologist to tackle the cichlids of Lake Victoria proper is Dr. Ole Seehausen. In August 1998, he published a paper describing 15 new species and erected three new genera, *Mbipia, Pundamilia,* and *Lithochromis,* to encompass most of his newly described species. In this same paper, he also redefined the genus *Neochromis.* He is one of the few ichthyologists qualified to study the cichlids of Lake Victoria in their multitude of complex and mystifying physical and behavioral parameters. He has also seen much validity in Greenwood's new genera. With some tweaking, he advocates their use when applicable. This philosophy is in keeping with Greenwood's sentiments since he was hoping to stimulate further discussion and work on the cichlids of the Lake Victoria basin by divvying them up into new genera. Therefore, the author aims to use the most correct generic names when known or assumed while leaving those species whose generic placement is unknown within the genus *"Haplochromis"* in brackets. As a result, Green-wood's desires have been realized as more and more work is carried out on this unique assemblage of cichlids from Africa.

Recent Changes in Cichlid Composition

Lake Victoria has received a great deal of press in the past several years due to the immense ecological deterioration that has transpired through the auspices of human activity, many of which seemed to have been well-meaning at the time. The most well-known alteration of the lake began when several Nile perch, *Lates niloticus,* were introduced into the northern side of the lake in Uganda in the early 1950s as well as into Lake Kyoga, with more following systematically in the 1960s. The purpose was to provide a viable fisheries industry in the lake. Such a mindset was not uncommon for fisheries personnel at this time around the world. In fact, attempts were even made later on to introduce Nile perch into Texas waters

Above: From the years 1984 to 1987, the population of many Lake Victoria cichlids collapsed, likely resulting in their extinction. One group hit particularly hard was the zooplanktivores of the genus Yissochromis. *Pictured is an undescribed species collected near Ulugi Beach at Rusinga, Kenya, that became extinct during this time.*

Above right: Pictured is another undescribed species of Yissochromis *that became extinct during the mid 1980s. This species was also collected offshore from Ulugi Beach at Rusinga, Kenya.*

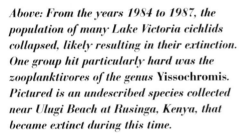

Right: Yet another undescribed species of Yissochromis, *referred to as Silver Bullet, that is now extinct. Pictured is a male collected offshore from Kangege Beach at Mbita, Kenya. This species was imported into the hobby, and it remains to be seen if any remain in captivity.*

officially, perhaps more so for sport fishing than for anything else. Thankfully, such efforts proved futile! The population of the Nile perch maintained a low profile until the early 1980s when their population exploded. The Nile perch can attain a length of around 6 feet (180 cm) and weigh nearly 300 pounds (135 kg). Since they are predatory by nature, the Nile perch preyed upon the endemic cichlid fauna of both lakes with gusto. The years 1984 through 1987 saw the cichlid population of the lake collapse, resulting in the extinction of over 200 species! The Nile perch's devastating effects upon Lake Kyoga has also been recorded. At least 30 species of piscivores have presumably become extinct since the perch's initial introduction. Fisheries catches were soon dominated by Nile perch, with a small percentage representing the endemic Haplochromines. Before the upsurge of the Nile perch, vast quantities of Haplochromines were caught annually, which provided much of the protein for the people living on or near the lake.

Nonnative Tilapiines were also introduced into the lake as a larger food fish. These nonnative species outcompeted the endemic species, *Oreochromis esculentus* and *O. variabilis*, causing their numbers to shrink to barely survivable numbers.

Another situation that has had a major effect upon Lake Victoria was the introduction of

The introduction of Oreochromis niloticus *into Lake Victoria caused the populaton of the less competitive native Tilapiines to shrink substantially. Pictured is a male caught on hook and line at Entebbe, Uganda.*

Yissochromis pyrrocephalus *is one of a few species that barely survived the Nile perch's ravenous appetite for small Lake Victoria cichlids. This species is making a comeback due to overfishing of Nile perch.*

water hyacinth (*Eichhornia crassipes*). It is believed to have been introduced into the lake in the late 1980s and since then has multiplied explosively. As of late 1998, it was said to cover 988,000 acres (400,000 ha) of water surface. As anyone who has grown water hyacinth can attest to, it grows at an incredibly fast rate. This

One of the few benefits that the introduction of the water hyacinth has brought to an already beleaguered Lake Victoria is a new source of refuge for juvenile cichlids.

has caused problems more for those who fish than for the cichlids themselves. In fact, the water hyacinth feeds on much of the raw sewage that is pumped daily into the lake from nearby cities. One of its few apparent benefits, at least to the Haplochromines, is that its dangling root masses provide a refugium for juvenile cichlids.

Another serious problem that has developed within Lake Victoria was the eutrophication of the lower two-thirds of the lake's depth. This situation is thought to result from the extinction of the phytoplankton-feeding cichlids, which was caused by the Nile perch and overfishing. Without this unique group of cichlids that fed upon the phytoplankton and kept it in balance, the phytoplankton increased beyond normal levels. This aided in robbing the lower reaches of the lake of oxygen, making the deeper parts of the lake completely anoxic, or devoid of oxygen, and incapable of sustaining fish life. Before the human-induced problems began to affect Lake Victoria seriously, oxygen

This freshly captured undescribed Haplochromine from Katwe Bay, Lake Edward is indicative of the attractive coloration and small size of many of Lake Edward's endemic species.

Xystichromis *sp. Dayglow Fulu was collected from Lake Kanyaboli, a small lake in Kenya a few miles east of Lake Victoria. Pictured is a male.*

It remains to be seen whether or not "Haplochromis" sp. Migori Red Chest is found in Lake Victoria proper. Thus far, it has only been collected from the Migori River, located just south of Winam Gulf in Kenya.

Astatotilapia latifasciata *is one of several species that have been collected from Lake Nawampasa, a small fingerlike lake connected to Lake Kyoga, in the past few years. Pictured is a male in full spawning dress.*

penetrated to the bottom of the lake. In fact, several species of cichlids were found exclusively in the bottom reaches of the lake. Such habitat-specific species are now presumably extinct. In addition to this, deforestation around the lake

has caused greater silting of the water from the effects of rainwater washing sediments into the lake, making it much less transparent than before. Lastly, some locals who fish have begun to place poisons into the water to catch certain

Second only to Lake Victoria, Lake Edward is home to more species of Haplochromines than any other body of water within the Lake Victoria basin. A view of Katwe Bay, Lake Edward.

Tilapiines. This, as can be readily assumed, also kills off the smaller Haplochromines and leaves behind toxins whose full effects upon the lake remain unkown. Some bays that have been heavily fished for Tilapiines are now assumed to be completely devoid of Haplochromines. This has been suggested for Butimba Bay in the Mwanza Gulf in southern Lake Victoria as a result of the use of chemicals.

Currently, the Nile perch is being seriously overfished, which may cause alarm for those relying upon its flesh as a commodity or to feed the local people. However, the overfishing has had a positive effect upon certain species because some are making a comeback. Once critically rare species are now common, such as *Yissochromis pyrrocephalus*. Whether those species that were considered extinct a few years

ago are still alive and are making a comeback remains to be seen.

In the Mwanza Gulf in the southeast part of the lake, two species of the genus *Yissochromis*, *Y. tanaos* and *Y. thereuterion*, made a complete location and habitat shift. Both species were common on the eastern side of the Mwanza Gulf from 1977 to 1981 at Butimba Bay. Afterward, none could be found at that bay. However, by late 1993, both species were found on the west side of the Mwanza Gulf, 5 miles (8 km) directly west of their old habitat at Kissenda Bay. Kissenda Bay has a muddy bottom and is rather exposed to the open waters of the gulf, whereas Butimba Bay has a sandy bottom and offers a more sheltered, quiet area. This being the case, it is entirely possible that many other presumably extinct species may have made radical habitat shifts and may occur in other, unexplored, or undersurveyed areas in small but nevertheless surviving numbers.

Between the years 1991 and 1995, extensive surveys were carried out in the Mwanza Gulf. The results indicated that 102 new species of Haplochromines were discovered for the first time, with about two-thirds of them found exclusively within rocky habitats. Other findings indicated that the rate of the cichlids disappearing slowed but was continuing nonetheless. Thankfully, most other bodies of water within the Lake Victoria basin have not been affected to the degree that Lake Victoria and Lake Kyoga have. Much still must be learned about the cichlids of the Lake Victoria basin. These small glimpses into an incredibly complex ecosystem are slowly helping to unravel the facts about these fascinating cichlids.

Lake Victoria Basin Cichlids in the Hobby

Today, many new species being collected and brought into the aquarium trade are found in the rocky habitats in very shallow water where the Nile perch has had less of an impact. Also, many Haplochromine species are being collected from the satellite lakes to the north, such as Lake Kyoga and Lake Nawampasa, Lake Kanyaboli to the east, Lakes Edward and George to the west, and in many of the rivers that pour out of or into such lakes. When new species are first imported into the hobby, exact collecting locality information is often lacking. This occurs partly because the local collector

wants to protect the collecting site from competitors. So the collector does not reveal the exact locality from where various Haplochromines are caught and exported for the hobby worldwide. Instead of giving an exact collecting site, some importers of these cichlids are willing to give only the country as the location. This, as can be expected from a group of cichlids that look very similar to each other, makes knowing if what one has is a cichlid from Lake Victoria proper or a species found in nearby neighboring lakes, swamps, or rivers exceedingly difficult.

From all indications, a vast number of undescribed species are apparently inhabiting the satellite lakes of Lake Victoria. For example, the tiny Lake Nawampasa, normally separated from Lake Kyoga by a narrow sandbank, is home to over three dozen species. Lakes Edward and George, connected to each other by the Kazinga Channel, are home to over 100 species of Haplochromines, a vast majority of which are scientifically undescribed at present! While visiting a small bay at Lake Edward in January 1994, this author was able to collect over 20 species of

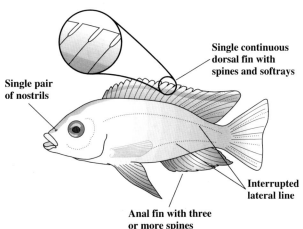

Single pair of nostrils

Single continuous dorsal fin with spines and softrays

Interrupted lateral line

Anal fin with three or more spines

External anatomy of a cichlid.

Haplochromines within a half an hour of collecting by using a small seine net in water less than 2 feet (60 cm) deep! Thus, a good number of new species being imported are not likely to have been collected from Lake Victoria proper.

History of the Lake Victoria Basin

Before Lake Victoria came into being, the geologic layout of the entire area was substantially different from what is seen today. What is now the present eastern shoreline region of the lake was, in the distant past, elevated to such an extent that water draining down the western side eventually flowed westward into Zaire and then into the Atlantic Ocean while water draining down the eastern side flowed toward the Indian Ocean. Later on, the area west of modern-day Lake Victoria rose up and caused the westward-flowing rivers to back up and overflow. The waters filled the valley-like depression between this newly formed western ridge and the older eastern one. Over time, the depression filled and became Lake Victoria. Since its inception, it has been a very unstable lake in terms of water depth and shoreline contour. During several important climactic time periods, the lake level rose and fell dramatically. At one time, this occurred so much so that three smaller lakes existed in what is now modern-day Lake Victoria. Perhaps the most dramatic change of all was when the lake completely dried up some 12,000 years ago! Since then, all the species in the lake have evolved into the several hundreds of different forms and species within that short span of time.

Lake Kyoga formed as Lake Victoria overflowed northward, with the rivers flowing through it backing up and forming this unusual, finger-shaped lake. Scientists have hypothesized that present-day Lake Kyoga looks like Lake Victoria did in the past as it was evolving and expanding.

In the early history of Lake Kivu, it existed as a much smaller, shallower body of water with its outlet draining northward into the area of Lakes

Edward, George, and Albert. This allowed for a free flow of genetic material between the two areas. At that time, Lake Victoria expanded westward to such an extent that it was in connection with the ancient Lakes Edward and George, also allowing for a free flow of genetic material. Eventually, a major geologic event transpired just north of Lake Kivu when the Bufumbiro volcanoes formed. This effectively blocked Lake Kivu's northward-draining river, forever severing its connection with Lake Edward. At this point, Lake Kivu filled with additional water and eventually found a southward-flowing valley to pour out of and into Lake Tanganyika via the Ruzizi River. Natural geologic barriers now prevent the cichlids of Lake Kivu and Lake Tanganyika from intermingling.

As the geology west of Lake Victoria began to rise, the lake became isolated from Lake Edward and Lake George. Today, Lake George is connected to Lake Victoria via the Katonga River. Whether any of the Haplochromines from Lake George find their way into Lake Victoria is difficult to say since extensive swampy areas are along this river. These may act as barriers, preventing the Haplochromines from moving between Lake George and Lake Victoria. Water flows north from Lake George via the Semliki River into Lake Albert. However, the cichlids of Lake George cannot migrate into Lake Albert because the Semliki Rapids act as a natural barrier to cichlid migration.

The rising geology west of Lake Victoria resulted in the permanent development of Lake Edward, which likely already had genetically similar cichlids to that of Lake Victoria at that time. A period may have transpired when the water level of Lake Edward was much lower than it is today. This would have meant that Lake George probably dried up completely sometime during its history due to its connection to Lake Edward via the Kazinga Channel. As the water level of Lake Edward rose, Lake George refilled and received new genetic material from Lake Edward.

General Facts

Lake Victoria, located in East Africa, is bordered by three countries. The southern half lies within the country of Tanzania, the northern half is in Uganda, and a northeastern wedge belongs to Kenya. Lake Victoria is around 240 miles (385 km) long and approximately 190 miles (305 km) at its widest point. It has a maximum depth of around 300 feet (90 m), however, a majority of the lake is less than 150 feet (45 m) deep. Since Lake Victoria is essentially a shallow, saucer-shaped lake with a large surface area and up until the human-induced effects descended upon the lake, the water column mixed completely. Oxygen was found all throughout the lake at all depths. Today, oxygen barely penetrates to a depth of 80 to 90 feet (25 to 28 m). The pH of the water is neutral to alkaline, ranging from 7.0 to 9.0, with a carbonate hardness of around 35 to 140 ppm. The temperature of the lake varies from 70°F to 81°F (21°C to 27°C), depending on the time of year. One last picture of the physical nature of the lake is the transparency of the water. When the water transparency was measured in the 1920s, it was around 27 feet (8 m) at offshore islands. As recently as the 1990s, the visibility at offshore islands was about 15 feet (5 m). Elsewhere, nearshore over muddy or sandy areas, the visibility can be as little as 3 feet (1 m).

The shoreline of the lake consists of extensive rocky areas, varying from beaches strewn with small pebbles to massive boulders piled up at the shore or jutting out of the water away from the shore. Between such rocky areas are sandy beaches or papyrus-fringed shorelines. As is the case in Lakes Tanganyika and Malawi, several submerged reefs as well as prominent islands are scattered throughout the lake. Some islands are so large they support whole communities of people. Others are small, rocky outcroppings large enough to serve as resting places for birds and homes for lizards and various insects. Several rivers pour into the lake. At these sites, much sediment covers any nearby rocks. Some aquatic plants are seen, particularly at such locations. For the most part, though, plants do not play a dominant role in the ecosystem of the lake in regards to the cichlid fauna. However, a couple of species of Haplochromines utilize plant matter as part of their diet.

Lake Kyoga lies completely within the country of Uganda and is located just north of Lake Victoria. Its overall diameter is around 70 miles (110 km) west to east and about 40 miles (65 km) south to north. It is essentially a river plain that overflowed and formed an unusually shaped, fingerlike lake with a multitude of tiny lakes and small swamps bordering its fringes. Perhaps the most well-known tiny lake that is ichthyologically part of Lake Kyoga is Lake Nawampasa. It is a small lake approximately 3 miles (5 km) long by 1 mile (1.6 km) wide, fringed with an abundance of various aquatic

Most of the shoreline of Lake George consists of extensive gently sloping sandy/muddy areas. View from the western side of Lake George at Hamukungu.

plants and surprisingly clear water. The maximum depth of Lake Kyoga is 20 feet (6 m), and it apparently has a greater concentration of minerals in the water than that of Lake Victoria.

Lake Kivu is bordered by Congo on the western half and by Rwanda on the eastern half. Today, this lake is well isolated from Lake Victoria. It is, in fact, the highest of the great lakes of Africa, with an altitude of around 4,500 feet (1,370 m) above sea level. It is around 35 miles (50 km) long and 20 miles (30 km) wide. It has a maximum depth of about 1,500 feet (460 m). However, only the upper 200 feet (60 m) of water is oxygenated. Maximum clarity has been recorded at 20 feet (6 m). The water has the unusual quality of having a large amount of dissovled carbon dioxide due to the magmatic nature of the bottom of the lake as well as methane produced from bacteria breaking down organic material. The water temperature averages around 76°F (24°C). Lake Kivu has a varied shoreline that alternates swampy areas containing abundant papyrus and water lilies with rocky shores that drop off steeply in some areas. Much of the rocks in the shallow areas of the lake are coated with a calcareous crust made from calcium carbonate and magnesium carbonate. It sort of acts as a glue, cementing the rocks together.

Lakes Edward and George are often treated together since they are connected by the Kazinga Channel, a 22-mile-long (36 km) river. Lake George is located within Uganda, while only the northeastern one-third of Lake Edward resides within Uganda. The remainder of that lake lies within Congo. The water from Lake George slowly flows down this channel and into Lake Edward. Lake George is approximately 9 miles (14 km) long by 11 miles (18 km) wide, while Lake Edward is approximately 57 miles (92 km) long by 30 miles (48 km) wide. Lake George has a maximum depth of 14 feet (4 m), while Lake Edward is nearly 380 feet (116 m) deep. Visibility is virtually nil in both lakes, and the pH of the water ranges from 8.7 to 9.9. The shorelines of these two lakes are essentially shallow, swampy areas with papyrus and water lilies, with no discernible rocky shorelines. The only exception to this is Kashaka Bay, a small, extinct volcano that connected to Lake George in the past. Between these two lakes, which share many of the same cichlid species, are probably more species of Victorian-like Haplochromines to be found than in any other body of water outside of Lake Victoria proper.

SETTING UP YOUR AQUARIUM

Before acquiring your first Lake Victoria basin cichlids, be prepared to invest your time to understand the basic husbandry requirements these cichlids will require. That way, you will meet with success the first time you set up your aquarium.

Aquarium Size and Shape

The habitat preference of Lake Victoria basin cichlids is either rock oriented, sand/mud bottom oriented, midwater/open water oriented, or a combination of two or all of these general habitats. The size and shape of the aquarium will be determined by the species you intend to maintain.

These cichlids are, by and large, naturally aggressive fish. When aggressive species are placed into the restricted confines of an aquarium, you are likely to see an increase in aggressive behavior, particularly if the aquarium is too small.

If you decide to maintain rock- or sand-/mud-oriented species, you should acquire an aquarium with a large amount of bottom space. Such an aquarium would provide more area to decorate the bottom of the aquarium adequately with rocks and/or sand, which helps

Java Fern, Microsorium pteropus, is an excellent plant for the Lake Victoria basin cichlid aquarium due to its tough leaves and low light requirements.

these species feel secure. On the other hand, if you decide to maintain midwater-/open water-oriented species, an aquarium that is more tall than wide would be better since many midwater-/open water-oriented species spend most of their time away from any substrate.

Giving precise instructions as to the size aquarium you should have for your cichlids is difficult, but a few guidelines can be suggested. Lake Victoria basin cichlids come in a wide range of sizes from which to choose. They range in size from a tiny, undescribed *Haplochromis* species that attains a length of 1 inch (2.5 cm) to the large, predatory species of the genus *Prognathochromis* and *Harpagochromis*, some of which can reach lengths of 12 inches (30 cm) and beyond. If you plan on maintaining the smaller species, such as species of the genus *Yissochromis* and some smaller *Astatotilapia* species, a small aquarium of approximately 30- to 40-gallon (110 to 150 L) capacity will suffice. For a great majority of Lake Victoria basin cichlids, whose average size is approximately 4 to 8 inches (10 to 20 cm), a far larger aquarium of approximately

Most Lake Victoria basin cichlids are aggressive by nature, so it is important to provide them with plenty of aquarium space. Pictured are two male **Pundamilia nyererei** *sparring over a contested territory.*

50- to 100-gallon (190 to 375 L) capacity would be prudent. By going to the other extreme, if you choose to maintain the largest species, such as some of the larger *Prognathochromis*, *Lipochromis*, and *Harpagochromis* species, an aquarium of at least 150 gallons (570 L) is recommended.

Approximately 0.5 inch (13 mm) of fish length per 1 gallon (3.8 L) of aquarium water is a good rule of thumb to follow. Be careful, however, in calculating this, since nearly all aquariums sold do not hold the exact gallons (liters) specified on the label. In order to calculate the volume of water in your aquarium properly, measure the inside of the aquarium in inches, multiply the length by the height by the width, and then divide by 231.

Another factor that will determine the size of your aquarium is the number of fish you plan on maintaining. Think ahead, and decide which species and how many of each you plan to maintain. Then acquire the appropriate aquarium size and shape.

The Aquarium Stand

Aquariums are heavy for their size. You must provide a sturdy, stable stand. Water weighs approximately 8 pounds per gallon (1 kg per 1 L). Added to the total weight of the water is the weight of the aquarium and the decorations in it. Not only does the stand need to be sturdy enough to handle all the weight, it also needs to be level so that no one area of the aquarium or stand receives more weight and pressure than necessary. If a stand or aquarium is not completely horizontal, placing a penny or two under the uneven portion of the stand or aquarium works well.

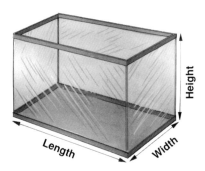

Mathematical equation for calculating the number of gallons of your aquarium: Measure the inside of the aquarium in inches, multiply the width by the height by the length, and then divide by 231.

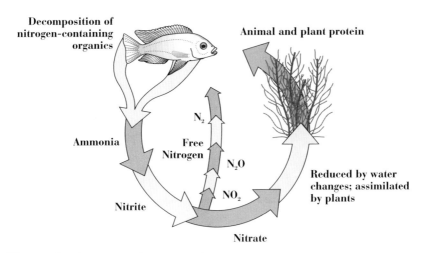

Decomposition of nitrogen-containing organics

Animal and plant protein

Ammonia

N₂
Free Nitrogen

N₂O

NO₂

Nitrite

Reduced by water changes; assimilated by plants

Nitrate

The nitrification process in an aquarium.

Types of Filtration

Filtration is perhaps the most important aspect of proper aquarium fish husbandry that needs to be understood before you can successfully maintain any fish in the restrictions of a captive environment. In order to maintain fish in an aquarium safely, their water must be filtered (processed). Three types of aquarium filtration are available. A combination of all three is ideal.

Biological filtration: The first and most important type of filtration is biological. This type is crucial to keeping fish in a closed environment—without it, maintaining fish in an aquarium is impossible. Any organic material, such as fish waste, uneaten food, decaying plant matter, or dead and rotting fish, is mineralized by heterotrophic bacteria, with the result that ammonia is produced. Ammonia is exceedingly toxic to fish. Additional bacteria further oxidize the ammonia into nitrite, and still other bacteria convert the nitrite to nitrate. This is the nitrification process, or biological filtration in its simplest form.

When you first install a biological filter, approximately four to six weeks are needed to grow enough bacteria to process your fish's

It is important to wait until the aquarium has cycled before adding your Lake Victoria basin cichlids, such as this male "Harpagochromis" sp. Blue Rock Hunter from Lake Victoria, into the aquarium.

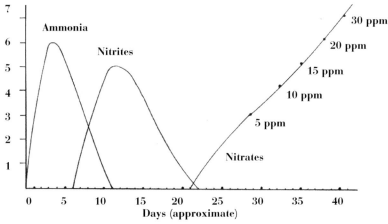

The cycling process of biological filtration.

excrement, uneaten food, and decaying plant matter efficiently. A common method employed to begin the four- to six-week maturation process is to use test fish. These can be any species of tropical fish that is extremely hardy and can withstand high concentrations of ammonia and nitrites. Some of the more commonly used, inexpensive, and hardy test fish are the paradise fish—*Macropodus opercularis* and the blue gourami—*Trichogaster trichopterus*. These labyrinth fish will normally survive the spike of ammonia and nitrite during the cycling process. Test fish should be maintained and fed daily in the newly set up aquarium until it has cycled. Do not perform any water changes during this period. After the aquarium has cycled, perform a 50 percent water change, remove the test fish, and add your prized cichlids.

A suitable way to follow the cycling process of your biological filter is to invest in test kits for ammonia, nitrite, and nitrate. Test your newly set up aquarium daily, and monitor any change that takes place. Alternatively, you can

have your water tested at any reputable tropical fish dealer. Over the course of the first few days, you will see a spike in the amount of ammonia in the water. As the ammonia recedes to negligible levels, the nitrites will spike, then the nitrites will slowly recede to negligible levels as you begin to get your first nitrate readings. When nitrites are no longer present, the aquarium has matured and the cycle is complete.

Biological filtration also produces hydrogen ions that lower the pH, making the water more acidic. The easiest way to combat this is to maintain a regular schedule of water changes. Frequent water changes will help to maintain a stable environment for your cichlids. In addition to preventing the water from becoming acidic, water changes will help to lower the nitrate levels. The overall well-being of your aquarium residents depends on regularly changing the water.

Chemical filtration: The second form of filtration is chemical, which may consist of carbon or various pelleted resins used to absorb harmful chemicals from the water. This type of filtration is useful if you live in an area where your local municipal water supply is contaminated with a variety of chemicals. Chemical filtration is also useful for removing medications from the water after medicines have effected a cure.

Mechanical filtration: The third form of filtration is mechanical. This form of filtration simply removes visible particulate matter as water passes through a filtering medium so that the water remains free of unsightly sediments.

Whatever form of filtration you decide to use, it should biologically filter the water in a consistent and adequate manner. It should also mechanically filter the water to remove visible organic material. Additionally, it should have the capacity to filter the water chemically to remove any harmful chemicals that may be present. You will need to make sure that the filter does not become clogged with organic material, thereby producing excessive amounts of nitrates. Servicing your filter and performing water changes on a regular basis will help to keep the nitrates low as well as prevent the water from becoming acidic.

Aquarium Water Chemistry

Lake Victoria basin cichlids hail from a variety of water quality parameters. Nevertheless, the water chemistry has a moderately high pH and alkalinity. Precisely duplicating the water chemistry where these cichlids naturally occur may be impossible. However, you can condition your aquarium water in the right direction and, in doing so, achieve a modest facsimile. The pH in the lake ranges from about 7.0 to 9.0 with a total mineral hardness of about 30 to 150 ppm of carbonate hardness (or 2 to 8

Remember to add water conditioner to all water being placed back into your aquarium. Otherwise, your cichlids may becomed stressed by the chlorine and other toxic chemicals usually present in municipal water. Pictured is a female Astatotilapia *sp. Red Tail from Lake Victoria.*

kH of German hardness). This makes the water neutral to alkaline with a moderate amount of mineral concentrations. Most municipal water comes out of the faucet with a pH of approximately 7.2 to 7.6 and a total mineral hardness that may vary substantially depending on your local water source. If your water parameters fall within the pH and hardness range of water from the Lake Victoria basin, the water can be used straight from the faucet. You should invest in test kits that measure for pH and water hardness or at least have your water tested at a local retail tropical fish establishment so that you will be able to determine whether your water needs buffering to increase the pH and kH. If your aquarium needs to be buffered to increase the pH and kH, a number of products are on the market that you can use.

The important thing to remember is that you should maintain consistency when using such products. Each time a water change is needed, additional lake salts to buffer the water backup should be mixed in with the new water before it is added back to the aquarium. If you choose to have gravel in the aquarium, a thin layer of crushed coral sand or oyster shells will probably be the substrate of choice since either material will continually leach out enough minerals to keep the water on the alkaline side. If your tap water is already alka- line and hard, an inert gravel such as silica sand may be used instead.

If you live in an area where your tap water has a relatively high pH and kH, nothing more needs to be done other than to add a water conditioner to remove any chlorine, chlo- ramine, heavy metals, and other contaminants. Remember to add water conditioner to all new water put into your aquarium.

Heater and Thermometer

Lake Victoria basin cichlids come from water with a temperature that ranges from 61°F to 82°F (16°C to 28°C). If you live in an area of the country that experiences very cold winters, then a heater will be needed to maintain the water temperature at a moderate level. If you live in an area of the country that experiences a mild climate all year-round, then a heater may not be necessary. Maintain the aquarium between 74°F and 78°F (23°C to 25°C). If your aquarium is too cool without a heater, then you must invest in a quality heater. Aquariums of up to 100 gallons (375 L) will probably need only one appropriately sized heater. Much larger aquariums should have two heaters, one at each end of the aquarium, for greater tem- perature stability. You will need to read the suggested heater size listed on the aquarium before purchasing a heater. It will give you a guideline regarding size and wattage needed

When maintaining Lake Victoria basin cichlids, such as this female **Harpago- chromis sp. Two Stripe White Lip** *in the aquarium, it is vitally important to have a quality filter.*

In order to observe your cichlids' activity levels at their best, maintain the aquarium water temperature between 74°F and 78°F (23°C and 25°C). Pictured is a male **Pundamilia nyererei** *from Ruti Island, Lake Victoria.*

The lighting in the aquarium should be somewhat subdued, in order that natural colors, as seen in this male "Haplochromis" sp. Migori Red Chest, will not be washed out.

"Haplochromis" sp. Black Silver Tip is a prodigious digger, so sand or gravel should be kept to a minimum, while rocks should be securely set up so that they will not fall over and damage the aquarium glass.

for your aquarium. A general guide to follow is about 3 watts per gallon (1 W per 1 L). For example, a 50-gallon (190 L) aquarium would need a 150-watt heater. The heater should be mounted in the aquarium only after it is full of water. Remember to allow about half an hour for the heater's internal thermostat to adjust itself to the temperature of the water before turning on your heater. At this point, install an accurate thermometer.

Lighting

Proper lighting enables you to observe your cichlids more clearly. The main lighting of choice is the fluorescent bulb. However, many Lake Victoria basin cichlids live in sediment-filled water in their natural habitat, so the amount of light that penetrates to their domain is substantially reduced. Only one bulb should therefore be used since too much lighting will wash out the colors of these cichlids and they

will simply not look their best. Choose those bulbs that give off white or daylight-quality lighting. Also, cichlids need to sleep as much as people do, so keep the lights on only during the day and turn them off at night.

Decorations

Determining what kind of decorations to use will depend on what species of Lake Victoria basin cichlid you plan to keep. As previously mentioned, these cichlids have three general habitat preferences: rock oriented, sand/mud oriented, and open water oriented. If you plan on maintaining rock-oriented species, several rocks should be piled up to form caves and passageways for the fish to find refuge in and to establish territories. Rocks should be relatively smooth. Jagged lava rocks should be avoided since they may injure your cichlids if the fish accidentally scrape against the sharp edges. Very little sand should be used, just

Yissochromis sp. Argens is a species that spends most of its time away from the substrate. This species is best maintained in an aquarium devoid of rocks.

enough to cover the bottom of the aquarium. The rock-oriented species are prodigious diggers and will pile up sand/gravel into unsightly heaps. If very large rocks are used, a small piece of Styrofoam can be placed underneath the sections of the rock that will be in contact with the glass. This will protect the bottom pane.

For the sand-/mud-oriented species, a shallow layer of fine silica sand is preferred. Only a few smooth rocks should be present, strategically placed so as to serve as territorial boundaries. These few rocks may also provide a degree of refuge from other fish and a greater sense of security in the restrictions of an aquarium.

For the open water-oriented species, a shallow layer of silica sand without any rocks will suffice. After all, these fish will be spending most of their time in the upper water column.

The background can be decorated with dark blue or black background sheets from your local tropical fish dealer. Prefabricated rock molds designed to be glued onto the inside back of the aquarium provide a realistic decoration for these cichlids.

Sand/Gravel

Most people want to have some sand or gravel in their aquariums. Not only is it pleasing to the eye, it hides the bottom of the aquarium from view. However, having too much sand or gravel will invite bacteria to form anaerobic conditions in the deeper recesses of the gravel bed, so not having too much is advisable. If you maintain an undergravel filter, a standard 2 inches (5 cm) of gravel depth will suffice. Barring this type of filtration, a fine layer of no more than 0.5 inches (1.3 cm) of sand or gravel will be enough. If you plan to maintain sand-/mud-oriented species, silica sand is ideal.

Live Plants

Live plants can add a nice finishing touch to the aesthetics of an aquarium. The primary place where plants are present in the Lake Victoria basin in any significant numbers are at river mouths and at some areas of shoreline where the water is laden with sediments. Many smaller lakes within the basin have extensive aquatic plants throughout all habitats. Whether you decide to have plants in your aquarium or not is a matter of personal taste. If you do wish to maintain live plants with these cichlids, maintaining those species of the genus *Vallisneria* and *Ceratophyllum* are recommended. Another popular aquatic plant that can be maintained with these cichlids is Java fern, *Microsorium pteropus*. This is a

"Haplochromis" sp. Gold Edward is an attractively colored, small species collected from Katwe Bay, Lake Edward. Upon being preserved, it developed several black vertical bars along the body. (See description on p. 64.)

This large, nearly seven-inch female Harpagochromis squamipinnis was captured in Kashaka Bay, Lake George. It is a brooding female with over 200 eggs in its mouth!

This female Lipochromis sp. Parvidens-like should not be housed with other similar looking Lipochromis species, since hybridization is likely to take place.

This variant of Paralabidochromis chilotes was collected from Kenyan waters. Pictured is a male.

tough species that loves moderate-to-hard water and can thrive on even somewhat reduced light levels. *Anubias* species will do well because they tolerate low light levels, have thick and tough leaves, and tolerate a wide range of water chemistry. If you maintain species that dig profusely, you will want to have a shallow bed of sand or gravel. Obtaining your plants in a potted form may be the best way to go. Most retail establishments sell their plants in plastic pots with a dense, fabriclike potting material. If you do not like to see the pot in your aquarium, you can easily cover it with a few small stones. You must remember that all live plants need some amount of sunlight or artificial lighting in order to thrive.

HOW-TO: TYPES OF FILTERS

Many types of filters are on the market. Most do a fair job at maintaining adequate water quality, but some are more efficient than others. Learn about the most popular types before you decide on the best one for your cichlids.

Undergravel Filter

Undergravel filters have long been a very popular filter for both saltwater and freshwater aquariums. A plate is placed under the gravel. Water is drawn down through the gravel by a submersible water pump or air-driven stone, pulled through the plate, and circulated back into the aquarium via a tube at the back end of the plate. Bacteria accumulate in the gravel bed so that the gravel bed becomes one big biological filter. These filters provide satisfactory biological filtration initially. Eventually, though, they become saturated with organic

material and so become nitrate-producing factories. They perform an average job at providing mechanical filtration and provide absolutely no chemical filtration. Organic material eventually translates into the production of nitrates through the nitrification process, so removing as much organic material as possible is important to keep nitrates to a minimum. With undergravel filters, this is nearly impossible. Over time, this type of filter will collect more organic material than you will be able to remove, particularly below the plates. This will result in the production of high levels of nitrates, regardless of frequent, large-scale water changes and gravel vacuuming.

Trickle Filter

The trickle filter is an excellent biological filter, particularly if you wish to filter large

aquariums. Oxygen saturation is achieved in this filter as the drops of water trickle through the ball-like filter medium. The prefilter serves as the mechanical portion of this filter. A small chamber is next to the filter medium in which to place chemical-filtering material. Over time, the plastic balls and other internal parts of the filter gather more and more organic material, which, in turn, produces large quantities of nitrates. If the plastic balls are occasionally flushed of their organic buildup and/or a small portion periodically replaced with new plastic balls, excessive amounts of nitrates should not be a problem. Also, as part of regularly maintaining any filter, you will need to examine the inside of the filter to make sure it is functioning optimally. You should remove any buildup of organic material from the walls and floor of the filter as well as from the intake and outtake tubes.

Canister Filter

Canister filters provide the three types of filtration already mentioned: biological, chemical, and mechanical. However, they require a lot of servicing if one is to keep the collection of organic material inside the canister to a minimum. They can be difficult

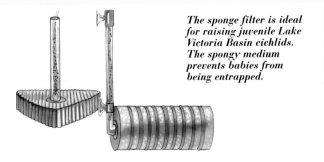

The sponge filter is ideal for raising juvenile Lake Victoria Basin cichlids. The spongy medium prevents babies from being entrapped.

and messy to clean, something that most people use as an excuse to put off regular maintenance. Keeping the prefilter clean is important in order to not impede water flow through the canister.

Box Filter

Box filters are capable of providing all three types of filtration but must be serviced frequently in order to keep organic material from building up to the point of producing large amounts of nitrates. Some hobbyists have modified box filters to contain only dime-sized lava rocks in the lower half of the chamber while having a thick piece of sponge on the top half of the chamber. The lava rock provides the surface space for nitrifying bacteria to colonize and thus provide for biological filtration. Simultaneously, the sponge serves primarily as a prefilter, reducing organic material buildup on the lava rocks. This type of filter seems to work best when the sponge is rinsed thoroughly once a week. It is ideal for aquariums no larger than 30 or 40 gallons (110 to 150 L).

Sponge Filter

Sponge filters are excellent for small aquariums and for raising juvenile fish. Their surface area is too small to entrap juvenile fish. Eventually, the sponge will break down and need to be replaced, so the process of reestablishing a biologically mature filter must start again. You can avoid this by starting up another sponge filter two months before replacing the old one.

Fluidized Bed Filter

Another filter on the market is the fluidized bed filter. This type is a more efficient biological filter than those previously mentioned. Unless a prefilter is attached to the intake valve of the fluidized bed filter, it will provide no mechanical

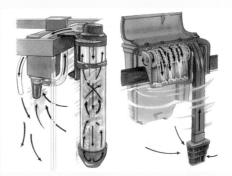

The fluidized bed filter (left) is one of the newest filters on the market; it provides excellent biological filtration. The biological wheel filter (right) is another excellent aquarium filter; it provides all three types of filtration in an efficient arrangement.

filtration. The fine sand in this filter will eventually clog, reducing its efficiency. It also does not provide any chemical filtration.

Biological Wheel Filter

The biological wheel filter provides all three types of filtration: biological, chemical, and mechanical. This type of filter can be quickly and easily cleaned of its organic buildup without compromising its biological filtering capabilities. This filter has a corrugated wheel situated in the pathway of the water return. As water is returned to the aquarium, it pours over the corrugated wheel, which, once mature, contains the bacteria necessary for biological filtration. This arrangement also enables oxygen to saturate the water, something needed not only by fish but also by the nitrifying bacteria. The back chamber of this filter provides for mechanical and chemical filtration in the form of a filter pad that can be easily replaced before it clogs with organic material.

MAINTAINING THE AQUARIUM

Once you have set up your Lake Victoria basin cichlid aquarium, you must regularly maintain it. By doing so, you will assure the long-term health of your aquarium inhabitants.

Water Changes

Changing water on a regular basis is the single most important task of keeping fish in an aquarium. Several factors will determine when, how much, and how often you should change your aquarium's water. The number of cichlids you are maintaining, the amount of food fed at each feeding, and how many times they are fed daily will all determine your water-changing routines. Approximately 25 percent of the volume of the aquarium's water should be changed weekly or 33 percent every two weeks in an aquarium that is sparsely populated (0.5 inches of fish per gallon [3 mm per 1 L]). If you crowd your cichlids (1 to 2 inches of fish per gallon [7 to 13 mm per 1 L]), then 40 percent water changes weekly or 60 percent water changes every two weeks should be standard procedure. These are rough guidelines to follow. You may need to change the water somewhat more or less depending on the number of fish and the quantity of food given.

As previously mentioned, you should invest in quality test kits. Once your biological filter has cycled, you will be testing primarily for nitrate levels, which will give you an indication when a water change is required. Ideally, your cichlids should not be exposed to nitrate concentrations beyond 20 ppm for extended periods of time. Many experts agree that long-term exposure to high nitrate levels weaken fish's immune systems. Most cichlids can survive high nitrate readings for a while, yet maintaining them in less-than-ideal water parameters over long periods of time is just asking for trouble. Cichlids kept in water with high nitrate levels over an extended period of time may become weakened and unable to

Top: If your existing aquarium is already fully stocked with Lake Victoria basin cichlids, then consider setting up another aquarium to house additional species, such as this **Paralabidochromis paucidens** *from Lake Kivu. Pictured is a young male collected from the eastern side of the lake in Rwanda.*

Bottom: It is difficult to give a clear food preference for some **Pundamilia,** *such as this dominant male* **Pundamilia nyererei** *from Ruti Island, since they consume a wide variety of foods in the wild.*

All species of Yissochromis *are considered to be more sensitive to improper water management than other Lake Victoria basin cichlids. Pictured is a male* Yissochromis pyrrocephalus *from Lake Victoria.*

You should purchase your Lake Victoria basin cichlids from reputable dealers that maintain their specimens in clean, low-nitrate water. Pictured is a subdominant male Ptyochromis xenognathus *from Lake Victoria.*

resist bacterial or parasitic infections. On more than one occasion, the author has seen cichlids go into shock and die within a matter of seconds while being spooked or netted out of an aquarium after having endured the strain of high nitrates over an extended period.

How can you know if your water changes are keeping the nitrates at an acceptably low level? Before each regular water change, test the water for nitrates. Then keep a log of the readings for several weeks. If the readings show that the nitrates are slowly increasing in spite of regularly changing the water, you will need to perform larger and/or more frequent water changes. You may also need to take special care to remove as much detritus as possible with each water change. If you have an undergravel filter in place or just have a thin layer of gravel without an undergravel filter, you will need to vacuum the gravel bed during each water change. If using box or power filters, this will likely entail removing the mechanical filtering

portion and rinsing off the accumulated detritus and/or throwing the filter away and replacing it with a new one. Lastly, you may also need to cut back on the amount of food you offer your cichlids. The key is to remove as much detritus from the aquarium as quickly as is reasonably possible. The end result of bacterial interaction with detritus is the production of nitrates. If the detritus is allowed to build up, it can truly produce a tremendous amount of nitrates, more so than you will be able to control through water changes alone. It is entirely possible that you can do as much as a 90 percent water change in an aquarium and, by the next day or so, have the nitrates up to their pre–water change levels if much of the detritus is not removed.

Acquire only healthy cichlids for your aquarium. Even if the species you want to purchase look outwardly healthy—no clamped fins and no scratching on rocks or plants—water quality may have elevated levels of nitrates in the dealer's tank. Some retail establishments, particularly large, supermarket-sized pet stores, often maintain their tropical fish in water with high nitrate levels. Asking what the nitrate level is before you purchase your cichlid might be advisable. Perhaps the water could be tested before a particular fish is purchased. Purchasing your cichlids from stores that maintain their specimens in clean, low-nitrate water is clearly preferable.

Siphoning water from the aquarium is the most efficient way to perform a water change. If the aquarium is large, siphoning the water out—via a garden hose—into the yard is recommended. For small aquariums, siphon the water into a bucket, then dispense with the water elsewhere. Always siphon from the bottom of the aquarium, particularly if you have an undergravel filter and are using a gravel vacuum.

The use of a siphon hose will be an invaluable piece of equipment for performing water changes. Water from the bottom of the aquarium should be siphoned out. If you have gravel or sand in your aquarium, a modified siphon hose with a wide mouth at the intake end is recommended. This widened end should be placed into the gravel or sand so that the siphoning action will lift the detritus out while leaving the substrate behind.

Any new water being placed back into the aquarium should first be thoroughly conditioned with water conditioner available from your local tropical fish dealer. The temperature of the new water should be the same as that of the aquarium water and never cooler.

Aeration

The aquarium water should be saturated with oxygen at all times. Not only do your cichlids need oxygen to survive, so do the bacteria in your biological filter. A clear sign that not enough oxygen is present in the water can be seen when your cichlids hang out near the top of the aquarium with their mouths touching the surface, gasping for what little oxygen is left. Making sure that enough oxygen is present in the water can be accomplished by the use of an airstone/air pump combination or an outside power filter trickling water back into the tank, agitating the surface.

Diet

In their natural habitat, cichlids of the Lake Victoria basin have been designed to specialize on a wide variety of foods. Some eat algae, fish, scales of other cichlids, snails, microinvertebrates, plants, crabs, shrimp, sponges, plankton, or mud. Interestingly, in captivity these cichlids will consume other kinds of foods for which they were not specifically designed. For example, piscivores of the genera *Prognathochromis* and *Harpagochromis* have been occasionally found to have algae in their stomachs! In captivity, they will not hesitate to consume algae flakes, fresh or frozen shrimp, or pelleted aquarium foods. Also, the rock-dwelling species of the genera *Lithochromis*, *Pundamilia*, and *Mbipia* consume such a wide variety of food items in the wild, such as filamentous algae, shrimp, plankton, sponges, aquatic insect larvae, and diatoms, that categorizing their clear food preference becomes difficult. (This may be due to the human-induced problems that have beset Lake Victoria. They have robbed the fish of their original food items, thus forcing the fish to consume other food items rather than starve to death). Thus, giving clear-cut categorizations to the cichlids of the Lake Victoria basin in terms of diet is difficult. On top of that, food preferences may be influenced by the sexual maturity of some of these cichlids. This is seen in the case of the Blue Nyererei, *Pundamilia azurae*, whose females and immature males show a preference for the algae on the rocks, while dominant, spawning males show a preference for plankton.

A large margin of flexibility in what sorts of foods are offered to the cichlids of the Lake Victoria basin is reasonable. Nevertheless, the foods that they consume in the wild should be simulated with a reasonable substitute. For those species that consume a large amount of algae, many high-quality flake foods are on the market with spirulina as a main ingredient. This food item makes for a great substitute for algae.

For those species that consume primarily small fish or shrimp, the source of protein

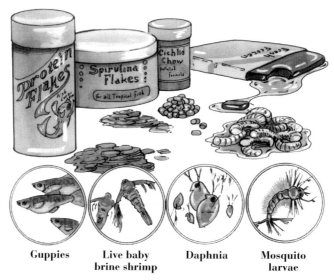

Guppies   **Live baby brine shrimp**   **Daphnia**   **Mosquito larvae**

A varied diet is important for the overall well-being of your Victoria Basin cichlids.

Some piscivorous Haplochromine species from the Lake Victoria basin, such as this **Harpagochromis** *sp. Pallisa Black Slick from Lake Nawampasa, have been known to occasionally ingest algae.*

For herbivorous species, such as this "**Haplochromis**" *sp. Ruby from Lake Nawampasa, that scrape off algae from aquatic plants, spirulina-based foods provide an adequate substitute for algae in captivity. Pictured is a male.*

should be aquatic and not mammalian. Mammal meat such as beef heart contains a high percentage of fat that can easily compact the digestive tract of your cichlids. Raw fish flesh, shrimp, or even disease-free feeder guppies are ideal. Name-brand, high-protein flake foods, pellets, and freeze-dried ocean plankton are all additional food items that you can offer.

For planktivorous species, such as those species of the genus *Yissochromis*, live or frozen daphnia, mosquito larvae, and live baby brine shrimp would be ideal. High-quality flakes, freeze-dried plankton, and small pellets can all be offered to round out their diets.

In regards to some unusual dietarily specialized species, such as the scale eater *Allochromis wellcommei* and many of the paedophores of the genus *Lipochromis* that engulf the mouths of brooding cichlids and suck out the larvae, feeding them their natural food items may not be feasible in captivity. However, they too will readily adapt to prepared

Even though this **Lipochromis** *sp. Parvidens-like from Lake Nawampasa specializes in feeding upon the eggs and larvae of brooding Haplochromines, it has shown itself to be quite flexible in captivity in regard to the foods it will consume. Pictured is a female.*

aquarium fish foods and live foods small enough to fit into their mouths.

Take extra care not to overfeed your cichlids. Overfed cichlids will not look their best, may become lethargic, may lose much of their natural colors, and may cease to show any interest in spawning. They might also grow to hideously large sizes as a result of being fed too much, sizes that they would never reach in the wild. Nothing is more repulsive than an overweight, oversized cichlid! Not giving your cichlids all they can consume in one feeding is always a good idea. If they are kept slightly hungry, they will always be on the prowl for food and displaying more natural modes of behavior.

The parasite ich is commonly encountered in Lake Victoria basin cichlids.

Parasites and Bacterial Infections

A whole multitude of parasites and bacterial infections are sporadically encountered in tropical fish, but only a couple seem to be recurrent problems with Lake Victoria basin cichlids. The easiest thing you can do to minimize the risk of your cichlids catching a particular ailment, be it a parasite or bacterial infection, is to practice good husbandry skills. These will assure a healthy environment for your cichlids that will, in turn, result in healthy, vigorous cichlids. Only when the needs of your cichlids are not being met do they begin to become stressed. The immune system of your cichlids weakens considerably when it becomes stressed and will not be able to fight off an encroaching parasitic or bacterial infection. The result may be that your cichlids develop a debilitating ailment that will need medicinal treatment if they are to survive. If they come down with parasites or a bacterial infection, the following tips may be helpful.

Ich, or *Ichthyophthirius multifilis*, is probably the most commonly encountered parasite to attack fish in the aquarium. It seems to rear its head when fish are stressed due to a sudden drop in temperature. This parasite may not manifest itself for several days and may attach itself only inside the gills of the host fish. If ich confines itself to the gills, it will be nearly impossible to detect at first. When ich attacks in this

Good husbandry practices help prevent bloat (top) and hole-in-the-head disease (bottom).

manner, your fish may eventually die, seemingly for no apparent reason. In fact, this is not uncommon. At other times, you will see tiny white dots sprinkled over the fish's body, something like the color and size of salt grains. In whichever region of the body the ich manifests itself, the affected fish will probably be seen to glance off objects in an apparent effort to scratch itself. Fortunately, this is one of the easiest parasitic infections to treat. Malachite green is the most readily available medicine one can use to treat ich. Ich has a three-day life cycle, so the medicine should be present in the water for at least three days, four to five being better. Remove any carbon from your filter before using the medicine since the carbon will absorb the medicine, rendering it ineffective. A slight rise in water temperature will help to speed up the life cycle of the ich and help the medicine effect a cure a little sooner. A 25 percent to 50 percent water change after the completion of treatment is advisable along with the addition of fresh carbon to absorb any residual medication that may still be present in your aquarium.

Bloat: Another ailment that commonly affects Lake Victoria basin cichlids, particularly those species that tend toward the herbivorous side, is bloat. Bloat is caused when the intestinal tract of the fish becomes infected/inflamed. The inflammation is usually caused by a combination of improper diet—feeding herbivorous species high-protein foods—and/or too much of the same kind of food followed by poor water quality. This condition, unless treated immediately, may result in the death of the fish within a few days. If treated immediately upon signs of first symptoms (loss of appetite, noticeable distention of the body region, and increased respiratory rate), a cure may be possible but is

Lake Victoria basin cichlids will likely come down with ich if stressed for extended periods of time, particularly if the water temperature is too cold. Pictured is a male of an undescribed "Haplochromis" species found in Winam Gulf, Lake Victoria.

not always guaranteed. The medication metronidazole is often used at ⅛ teaspoon (0.6 mL) per 20 gallons (75 L) of water once a day for three to five days. After completing the treatment, perform a 50 percent water change and add carbon to the filter to absorb any residual medication. Again, prevention is the best strategy. The author strongly urges you to feed the proper foods, taking particular care not to overfeed as well as to maintain a clean aquarium.

Fin rot: The bacterial infection called fin rot is evidenced by frayed fins that look as though they have deteriorated away. Fin rot can be treated with any medication on the market that has the drug furazolidone as its active ingredient. Be sure to follow the directions on the package carefully.

Eye infections: Several large-eyed Lake Victoria basin cichlids may be prone to developing eye infections. This usually begins when the cichlid scratches its eye against a sharp object in the aquarium. The infection invariably takes hold when the water quality is poor and the injured cichlid has been stressed for some length of time. Medications on the market are specially designed to treat eye infections. They have silver nitrate as the active ingredient. The medication must be applied to the infected eye twice a day. Unfortunately, this means that the fish needing treatment must be removed from the water. This is a difficult condition to treat, and a cure is not always achieved.

Hole-in-the-head, or lateral line disease, may be caused by an infestation of flagellate protozoans attacking the sensory pores of a fish's head as well as its lateral line. This is indirectly brought on by poor husbandry practices and/or improper diet. Cichlids with this infection show pitting on the sides of the face and on the lateral line system on the sides of the body. Some species seem to be more prone to developing this malady than others. You can

It is important not to house large-eyed species, such as this Astatotilapia piceatus, *in an aquarium with sharp, jagged objects, since these species may end up injuring their eyes.*

keeps its occurrence down to a minimum by maintaining scrupulous aquarium conditions and making sure that your cichlids are being fed a well-balanced diet. Metronidazole may stop it from spreading. However, once the damage has been done, the pitting on the face and lateral line of the cichlids will always be present in the form of a scar. Oftentimes, nothing will stop the spread of the disease and the only thing that can be done is to euthanize the infected fish.

Quarantine and Hospital Aquarium

A method often employed by hobbyists and professionals alike is the use of a quarantine aquarium to house newly acquired fish. Cichlids may be stressed and may carry a bacterial infection or have acquired internal or external parasites in the dealer's holding tank. If they were to be placed directly into your main aquarium with your other cichlids, the newly introduced cichlid might infect the other aquarium inhabitants. This can be a very frustrating experience and is one that we all have gone through as novice aquarists. A quarantine aquarium need only be a 10-gallon (40 L) aquarium. It should have a biological filter up and running such as an outside power filter or inside sponge filter but have no chemical filtration. A heater and thermometer is needed to maintain a constant temperature of 80°F (27°C). No gravel should be in the aquarium since it will make keeping the aquarium clean during treatment more difficult. The aquarium should not be lit overhead. Enough shelter should be placed into the aquarium so that the quarantined fish will feel safe and secure. If the fish is stressed because it cannot find a place to hide, it may not respond as quickly to treatment.

With a quarantine aquarium set up and running properly, any newly acquired fish should be placed into it for approximately one month. During this time, the quarantined fish is cared for in the same manner as you would with any other aquarium fish. If the fish does have a bacterial infection or parasites, then it will become apparent within a month's time. At first sign of such ailments, the quarantined fish should be treated with the proper medication until it is completely cured. Only then should it be placed into the main aquarium. To remove any leftover medication that may still be present in the quarantine aquarium, carbon (chemical filtration) should be added to the filter.

The quarantine aquarium may also double as a hospital aquarium for cichlids in your main aquarium that become injured or come down with an infection. This way, instead of treating the main aquarium, the fish in question can be removed and placed into the hospital aquarium for individualized treatment.

A quarantine aquarium can also serve as a hospital aquarium, where injured or diseased species can be kept for rest or treatment. Pictured is a female **Astatotilapia** *sp. Spot Bar from the Kenyan side of Lake Victoria.*

Adding New Cichlids into an Established Aquarium

If you want to add new cichlids to your aquarium, make sure that plenty of room and open territories are available for more fish. This may not always be possible considering the territorial nature of most cichlids of the Lake Victoria basin. Oftentimes, a newly introduced species will become bullied, sometimes to the point of death, because the other inhabitants have already had time to establish themselves and acquire territories. The new fish, without any territory in a new environment, is automatically placed at the bottom of the pecking order. You can rearrange the decorations when you add a new fish and, in this way, give all the cichlids an equal chance at procuring and establishing a territory. Alternatively, when you first stock your aquarium with these cichlids, do so all at once. That way, all the fish will become equally established. If you want to acquire additional fish and your existing aquarium is already firmly established, then consider setting up another aquarium or two.

SPAWNING TIPS FOR LAKE VICTORIA BASIN CICHLIDS

Beginning with quality specimens that you desire to breed is critical. Choose only those specimens with the best coloration and fin and body shape. The genetic integrity of captive Lake Victoria basin cichlids is crucial if they are to be maintained long term.

Setting the Groundwork

One rewarding facet of maintaining cichlids of the Lake Victoria basin is inducing them to spawn. The first step is to decide which species of cichlid you wish to try, taking into consideration your aquarium limitations and available funds. Then set out to acquire specimens. A reputable tropical fish dealer or specialty cichlid club are two sources that may offer some

Top: Some hobbyists choose to acquire wild specimens when gathering stock for spawning purposes. Pictured is a wild male Paralabidochromis sp. Rock Kribensis from the Ugandan side of Lake Victoria.

Bottom: Make every attempt to avoid inbreeding your cichlids. Prolonged inbreeding will result in a higher percentage of malformed individuals, such as this deformed male Ptyochromis sp. Hippo Point Salmon.

of these cichlids. Some hobbyists choose to purchase wild-caught adults, while others use captive-raised juveniles.

Avoid Inbreeding

Spawning brother to sister is often practiced among those who reproduce cichlids in captivity. It is an easily overlooked situation that should be guarded against. If several juveniles of a particular cichlid are purchased, the odds are that they all came from the same spawn. These juveniles are then raised up and allowed to pair off and spawn. The juveniles from the union of brother and sister are then sold or traded off to the next person who then repeats the process. You can begin to see how quickly the genetic integrity of a particular species will deteriorate if this scenario continues.

You can do two things to minimize this often repeated practice of inbreeding. The first is to work with wild-caught specimens. If you are not able to afford or find wild-caught specimens, the second option is to obtain high-quality, captive-bred stock. High-quality, captive-bred cichlids are those with the color and body shape closely matching that of wild-caught specimens. When obtaining captive-bred juveniles, make an effort to buy one or two specimens from different sources so that the likelihood of spawning brother to sister will be greatly diminished. Every effort to propagate wild-caught or high-quality, captive-bred stock is crucial with Lake Victoria basin cichlids.

Selective breeding is of primary importance in working with the cichlids of the Lake Victoria basin, particularly with those species that are extinct in the wild and survive only in captivity. These cichlids have the propensity to spawn early on at a young age, oftentimes typically before the hobbyist thinks they are ready for such reproductive activities. If you begin with several captive-raised young of a particular

Selective breeding of critically endangered species, such as this **Harpagochromis** *sp.* *Two Stripe White Lip, that exist only in captivity is of utmost importance in order to assure long-term survival.*

species, what may transpire over time is a spawning pair or colony where the male is several times larger than the females. Once a female begins producing eggs, much of her food intake goes to egg development, and she will not grow as quickly as a male. As a result, the male far outgrows the female. This situation may cause difficulty in maintaining these fish together in the same aquarium since the aggressive tendencies of the male may overwhelm the much smaller females. This can be overcome by separating the males from the females while still young and giving the females around one year to develop firmly into a larger mature size before placing them together with the male. Another possibility is to provide a lot of rocks piled up to form caves and areas of refuge for the females so that they will not be overly harassed by the dominant male.

Prevent Hybridization

Maintain whatever species you intend to spawn separate from other species. Do not mix two or more species of these cichlids together in the same aquarium if you intend to spawn them since they will likely hybridize. In fact, the Haplochromine cichlids of the Lake Victoria basin are so closely related to each other genetically that nearly any two species have the capacity to hybridize and produce fertile offspring capable of reproducing. Whatever the reasons are for this, the natural barriers in the wild that prevent hybridization on a massive scale are usually absent in the confines of the home aquarium. Maintaining more than a single species together in the restricted confines of the aquarium will make hybridization a real possibility.

Oftentimes, distinguishing between females of two or more similarly related species can be nearly impossible. If they are allowed to cohabitate together in the same aquarium, it will be nearly impossible for you to tell which female belongs to which male. If a spawning takes place, the only way for you to determine that the right male spawned with the right female is to grow up the juveniles and see what they look like while all the time keeping the female separate from the others until the matter can be resolved. The last thing that is needed are hybrid Lake Victoria basin cichlids making their way through the hobby or scientific institutions. So, do yourself a big favor, and maintain a group of only one species together for the purposes of spawning. If you desire to have a community aquarium of these cichlids, then consider maintaining an aquarium of only males.

In the wild, the cichlids of the Lake Victoria basin have an approximate three-year life span. However, in captivity and over several captive generations, their life spans may nearly double. For those species that live for a relatively Methuselah-like age, they may show evidence of a curved back and perhaps a hollow-looking stomach. With such extended life spans in captivity, these cichlids' reproductive careers are typically longer than in the wild. So, if in the wild, they reproduce for a little over 1½ years, in captivity they may double that reproductive period, provided that they are being maintained in an ideal condition in terms of water quality and diet. As a result, they have the capacity to produce more offspring than they normally would under wild conditions. This will invariably result in a greater number of potentially deformed juveniles or those with weak

Lake Victoria Basin cichlids will readily hybridize in captivity if given the opportunity. Great care should be exercised to prevent such accidental crossbreeding, as is seen in this hybrid between an unidentified "Haplochromine" species and a Paralabidochromis chilotes.

Yissochromis *sp. Argens lives in the open waters of Lake Victoria. The ideal spawning aquarium for this species should have a thin layer of sand, plenty of open space, and no rocks. Pictured is a male in spawning dress.*

In order to prevent overly aggressive males, such as this **Labrochromis ishmaeli**, *from killing unreceptive females, employing the divider method may be an option. Pictured is a male in spawning dress.*

Habitats for Spawning

For rock-oriented species, the landscape of the aquarium should consist of a large number of rocks piled up to form passageways and places of refuge. Territories will be formed in and around the rocks. Spawning will more likely occur in the rocks than elsewhere.

For the sand- and open-water-oriented species, the layout of the aquarium should be as open as possible. Only a thin layer of sand and a couple of smooth stones to establish boundaries and provide some security to a brooding female need be included. Aquatic plants may add an additional sense of security and help to reinforce territories.

colors or improper color patterning. Such progeny should not be permitted to spawn, thereby passing on their genetically inferior traits into the captive population.

Difficult-to-Spawn Species

Some naturally aggressive species may prove a real challenge to spawn in captivity. Dominant males may end up killing other males, unreceptive females, or brooding females if not enough hiding places are provided. In some circumstances, no amount of hiding places will prevent particularly aggressive males from wrecking havoc. This can be a real challenge if you have your heart set on maintaining and spawning a particularly aggressive species. Fortunately, you can do a couple of

An aquarium divider is a practical way to spawn highly aggressive Victoria Basin cichlids. The holes in the divider permit the male to fertilize the female's eggs, while at the same time preventing the male from overly harassing, or even killing, the female.

Top: The bulge in the throat of this female **Ptyochromis** *species indicates that it recently spawned.*

Middle: After you have removed the eggs or embryos from a brooding female, she may be placed back into the same aquarium, or into another aquarium to recuperate from the removal procedure. Pictured is a female Astatotilapia *sp. Spot Bar.*

Bottom: Live baby brine shrimp are an ideal food for juvenile Lake Victoria basin cichlids, particularly for those species that have red, orange, or yellow pigment, such as this male Astatoreochromis allauadi *collected from Lake Nawampasa.*

things to minimize the aggression and encourage successful spawning.

Crowd your aquarium with the species you wish to work with and remove all possible hiding places. This will have the effect of spreading out the aggression of the dominant male so that it does not focus on any one fish. If faced with too many of its own kind to chase after, the dominant male might become more mellow with this arrangement. However, give close attention to maintaining good water quality. Stocking an aquarium to its limits is risky and will result in greater quantities of waste being produced. The buildup of waste products must be dealt with by significantly increased water changing and frequently examining, cleaning, or replacing the disposable filter pad of your filter to make sure it is functioning capably.

Divide the aquarium into two with a single male on one side and a single female on the other side. An egg crate, which is a light-diffusing ventilated panel, works well. It can be found in the lighting department of your local hardware store. When the pair is ready to spawn, they will do so next to the divider. The male's sperm will easily pass through the divider and fertilize the female's eggs. The

Even though live baby brine shrimp are ideal for your juvenile cichlids, the adults of several species will consume them as well. Pictured is a female "Haplochromis" sp. Black Silver Tip.

female can then brood her clutch of eggs without being molested.

Raising Juvenile Cichlids

One of the best foods for juvenile cichlids is live baby brine shrimp, *Artemia nauplii.* They are easy to hatch out and make an excellent first food. Brine shrimp eggs can be obtained through your local tropical fish dealer or from specialty companies that advertise in aquarium-related magazines. Finely crushed flake food can also be offered in addition to the live baby brine shrimp. After feeding your juvenile cichlids, any uneaten food or waste on the bottom of the aquarium should be

siphoned out on a daily basis. As the fish grow and consume more food, the young fish must become accustomed to larger, more frequent water changes of 25 to 50 percent weekly.

Setting Up a Continuous Supply of Live Baby Brine Shrimp

1. Cut four empty 2-liter soda bottles according to the illustration.

2. Invert the longer cut bottles and place them upside down into the shorter cut bottles. Make sure that the lids on the inverted bottles are firmly in place.

3. Fill both inverted containers with water and add 2 to 3 tablespoons (30 mL to 45 mL) of rock salt to each. Insert the rigid tubing, connected to an air pump with flexible tubing, into each container all the way to the bottom of the inverted container.

4. Add 1 teaspoon (5 mL) of brine shrimp eggs to one container only.

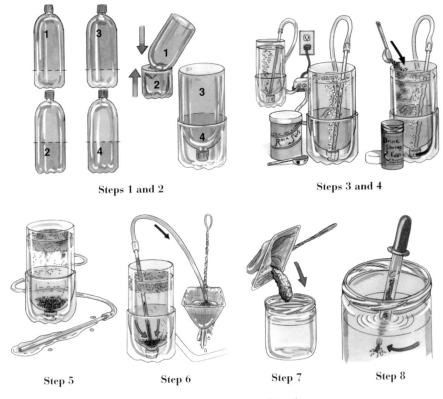

Steps 1 and 2

Steps 3 and 4

Step 5   **Step 6**   **Step 7**   **Step 8**

Hatching brine shrimp eggs (see illustration and text).

5. Wait 36 to 48 hours until the water takes on an orange cast. At this point, remove the rigid tubing and allow the eggs and shrimp to settle. The live baby brine shrimp will settle to the bottom of the container.

6. Take another piece of rigid tubing attached to flexible tubing. With the rigid end, siphon the live baby brine shrimp from the bottom of the container into a baby brine shrimp net.

7. Pour the live baby brine shrimp from the baby brine shrimp net into a small container of water.

8. By using an eyedropper, dispense the live baby brine shrimp from the small container.

One day after the first container of brine shrimp eggs hatch, begin the second container by following steps 4 through 8. One day after this second container hatches, rinse out the first container and start a new batch as you begin to dispense the live baby brine shrimp from the second container. Repeating this procedure will give you a constant supply of live baby brine shrimp for your juvenile Lake Victoria basin cichlids.

The most rewarding way to obtain offspring from parental cichlids is to let them do what comes naturally. One of the most satisfying experiences you will have in spawning Lake Victoria basin cichlids will be to observe and study the behavior of parents and juveniles. A time may come when you may want to separate the babies from a brooding female or from the main breeding aquarium and raise them on their own. This may occur particularly when the number of juveniles begins to crowd the aquarium or if the juveniles are being consumed by the other aquarium residents.

Removing Juveniles to a Separate Aquarium

If you opt to let the brooding female hold to full term in a community aquarium, the juveniles will likely be released to find refuge among the rocks. At this point, the only practical way to remove them from the aquarium is to remove all the rocks and carefully net the juveniles out, one by one. If you have a large, sparsely populated aquarium, consider letting the juveniles grow up alongside the adults. Many will be consumed along the way, but a few will grow to adulthood.

Most hobbyists choose to strip a brooding female or to remove it to another aquarium. Try removing the brooding female while she is asleep. Gently prod the brooding female into a shallow container or jar. Once in the container, place the female into another previously set up aquarium (preferably 10 gallons [40 L]) where the female can brood her young to full term and release them unmolested. This separate aquarium should be furnished with ample hiding places so that the brooding female feels secure.

Removing Eggs or Juveniles from a Brooding Female

You will know that a spawning has taken place when you see one or more females with a bulge in their throats, indicating that they are incubating a clutch of eggs. If you wish to save most of the spawn, many hobbyists choose to strip the female of her eggs and hatch them artificially. The most trouble-free way to catch the female is while she is asleep. Wait until the lights have been out for several hours, then turn on the lights and immediately catch the female with a net before she wakes up. This way, the female will not panic. Gently hold the female with one previously wetted hand. With a sharpened pencil in the other hand, carefully pry open her mouth, gently shaking the female in and out of the water while holding her over the net. The developing embryos or juveniles should begin to trickle out into the net. Continue this process until they have all been expelled from the female's mouth. Afterward, return the female to the breeding aquarium or place her into another aquarium to recuperate if needed. If juveniles are released, quickly place them into the grow-out

With wet hands, gently hold the brooding female in one hand. With a pencil in the other, carefully pry open its mouth over the parents' aquarium with a net in place. After the juveniles have been released from the female's mouth, the babies can be transferred to a grow-out aquarium.

FROM PARENTS

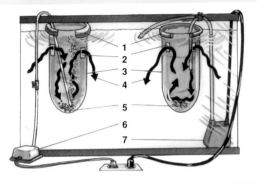

Two types of artificial incubators for mouthbrooding cichlid eggs.

1. *flotation device*
2. *vents*
3. *inverted plastic soda bottle*
4. *water current*
5. *embryo eggs*
6. *air pump*
7. *water pump*

aquarium that you have prepared beforehand with water from the parents' aquarium. If embryos are released, proceed to the next step of artificially incubating them.

Artificial Incubation

A typical incubator for mouthbrooding cichlid eggs or embryos consists of a small container set up inside an aquarium that, by means of aeration or gentle current, keeps the eggs in constant motion. This permits the proper development of the eggs or embryos into free-swimming juveniles. The container should be clear so that you can monitor the development of the embryos. After you have stripped the female of her clutch, the eggs or embryos should be immediately placed into the incubator. You will be able to ascertain when they become free-swimming when they have absorbed their yolk sacs and look like tiny fish. Once they have reached this stage, they can be

released from the incubator. You may want to place the incubator inside the grow-out aquarium in order to minimize the stress of transferring the juveniles to the grow-out aquarium.

If you wish to set up the artificial incubator in the grow-out aquarium, it should have the same water conditions and temperature as that of the parents' aquarium so that the eggs or embryos will not have to adjust to any change in water quality or temperature during their transfer and will not go into shock from the initial move. The grow-out aquarium (a 10-gallon [40 L] aquarium is ideal) should not have any decorations or gravel.

A sponge filter should be used since it will not ensnare the juveniles. It provides adequate biological filtration. However, you must remember that it will need between four and seven weeks to cycle and function properly before the juveniles are placed into the aquarium.

A REPRESENTATIVE SELECTION OF LAKE VICTORIA BASIN CICHLIDS

The cichlids of the Lake Victoria basin bear a close resemblance to one another due to their common ancestry. As such, many species currently in the hobby and assumed to have come from Lake Victoria proper are, in fact, found only in neighboring lakes, swamps, or rivers. The following representative selection is a testament to that fact.

Putting together a compilation of photographs and information on Lake Victoria basin cichlids is, by its very nature, a daunting task. Little has been published on the cichlids of this region of Africa. The information currently circulating is often revised or challenged by proceeding publications. The few books on the

Top: **Astatoreochromis allauadi** *is found not just in Lake Victoria, but also in most of the rivers and smaller satellite lakes within the Lake Victoria basin. Pictured is a male collected from Lake Nawampasa. (See description on pp. 56–57.)*

Bottom: Known as the Zebra Obliquidens in the hobby, **Astatotilapia latifasciata** *hails from Lake Nawampasa, a fingerlike lake projecting from Lake Kyoga. (See description on p. 58.)*

market dealing with these cichlids tend to be narrowly defined in terms of the region covered or the category of cichlid defined. Much of the Lake Victoria basin has yet to be systematically explored and its cichlids categorized.

Of all the bodies of water within the Lake Victoria basin, Lake Victoria has had the most research conducted on its cichlid fauna, particularly in the southeast part of the lake at the Mwanza and Speke Gulfs. Early work done by Greenwood focused primarily on those species found in the northern half of the lake. Lake Kivu and Lake George have been thoroughly explored in terms of determining their cichlid fauna. Lake Edward has been cursorily surveyed in conjunction with Lake George's comprehensive survey. Surveys on Lake Albert are all but nonexistent. Lake Kyoga has been largely overlooked. However, it is recently receiving some attention, especially since several of its tiny fringing lakes and swamps have been shown to house extant populations of cichlids formerly found in Lake Kyoga proper, the most well-known of these being Lake Nawampasa. This author's aim, therefore, is to give a brief overview of the cichlids of the Lake Victoria basin based upon information pulled together from a variety of sources.

Attempting to assertain precise collecting locality data and the range of a particular species is often difficult. Two reasons come to mind why this is so. The first is that private hobbyists may venture to this area of Africa and collect a species or two from a nearby stream or at the edge of one of the satellite lakes or swamps without knowing the name of the body of water or exactly where they are collecting. The second reason may be that local collectors, desiring to protect their source of income, will not divulge the exact locality from where their fish were caught other than giving the name of the country where it was found. Added to that are trade names, given to new species or color variants, that may change by the time the fish has made its way to the hobbyist's aquarium.

Another daunting situation to grapple with is that several Lake Victoria basin cichlids have the propensity to produce a variety of color mutations. Probably the most common color mutation observed among these cichlids in captivity is black. Several very distinctively colored species may all sport black mutations (usually in the males), causing many species to look virtually identical to each other. Also, the question of whether or not one is dealing with a mutation becomes blurred since many species begin life with colors typical for the species only to change to an entirely black coloration when older. Thus, if one is attempting to identify a black-pigmented species without any point of reference to go by, it may be nearly impossible to identify, especially if the species in question has no distinguishing physical features to set it apart.

If some question exists as to the identity of a particular species, the designation "cf." before the species name will indicate that the cichlid in question is closely related to or should be compared with the species whose name is used. Any genus name with quotes indicates that the species will likely be placed into a newly erected genus upon further scientific analysis. The cichlids of the Lake Victoria basin are referred to in the hobby largely by their scientific names and, to a lesser extent, by their common names. However, the use of scientific names is necessary. Whenever a species is also known by one or more common names, such name(s) will follow the current scientific or trade name. The cichlids of the Lake Victoria basin are in a state of taxonomic flux. Therefore, some genera that several species are catagorized under may change over time as additional scientific work is carried out. Also, invalid or misapplied scientific names are listed in this part when applicable. A brief discussion is included for all the species covered. Information is presented on the name, location and natural habitat, adult size, husbandry requirements, diet, and breeding of each species.

Name: *Astatoreochromis allauadi*
Location and Natural Habitat: Found throughout the Lake Victoria basin in lakes, rivers, and swamps. Inhabits shallow, papyrus-filled areas near the shore.

Adult Size: To 6 inches (15 cm).

Husbandry Requirements: Best maintained in aquariums no smaller than 50 gallons (190 L). Provide a few hiding places such as smooth stones, hardy aquatic plants, or other smooth structures. Several males and females can be housed together without too much difficulty.

Diet: Omnivorous, but those specimens from Lake Victoria primarily eat mollusks. Offer a variety of high-protein foods such as fresh and frozen chopped clams or mussels and commerically prepared tropical fish foods. Supplement the diet with spirulina flakes.

Breeding: A maternal mouthbrooder. Males establish territories among the rocks or out in the open over sandy substrates, and spawning occurs within the male's territory. A brooding female will seek refuge to brood her eggs. Feed juveniles live baby brine shrimp and finely crushed spirulina flakes.

Astatotilapia elegans is another commonly encountered species near the shoreline. Pictured is a male from Katwe Bay, Lake Edward.

spawning occurs within the rocks of the male's territory. A brooding female will seek refuge among the rocks. Feed juveniles live baby brine shrimp and finely crushed spirulina flakes.

Name: *Astatotilapia aeneocolor* (see photo on p. 55).

Location and Natural Habitat: Lake Edward and Lake George. Found along the shoreline in shallow, muddy water.

Adult Size: To 5 inches (12.5 cm).

Husbandry Requirements: Best maintained in aquariums no smaller than 50 gallons (190 L). Provide a few hiding places such as smooth stones, hardy aquatic plants, or other smooth structures. Several males and females can be housed together amicably.

Diet: Feeds on detritus, including insect larvae, adult insects, and plant fragments. Offer a variety of aquarium foods. Diet should be supplemented with spirulina flakes and live brine shrimp.

Breeding: A maternal mouthbrooder. Males establish territories among the rocks, and

Name: *Astatotilapia elegans*

Location and Natural Habitat: Found in Lakes Edward and George as well as the Kazinga Channel. Inhabits the shallow, nearshore areas among reed beds.

Adult Size: To 4 inches (10 cm).

Husbandry Requirements: Best maintained in aquariums no smaller than 40 gallons (150 L). Provide a few hiding places such as smooth stones, hardy aquatic plants, as well as plenty of open sandy areas. Maintain in a group of at least six individuals.

Diet: Feeds on aquatic insect larvae in the wild. Provide a varied diet high in protein such as krill, brine shrimp, pellets, and flakes. Supplement the diet with live baby brine shrimp, bloodworms, and mosquito larvae.

Breeding: A maternal mouthbrooder. Males establish territories among the rocks or reeds, and spawning occurs within the male's territory. A brooding female will seek refuge among the rocks. Feed juveniles live baby brine shrimp and finely crushed spirulina flakes.

Name: *Astatotilapia latifasciata*, Zebra Obliquidens

Location and Natural Habitat: Found in Lake Nawampasa and Lake Kyoga. Lives among the aquatic plants surrounding the perimeter of the lake.

Adult Size: To 4-1/2 inches (11.5 cm).

Husbandry Requirements: A relatively peaceful, solitary species that should be housed in aquariums no smaller than 50 gallons (190 L). Can be maintained with other species of Victorian Haplochromines provided it is not bullied by larger species. Provide a few hiding places such as smooth stones, hardy aquatic plants, or other smooth structures. Several males and females can be housed together amicably.

Diet: In the wild primarily an insectivore, but the diet ocassionally includes fins and

Astatotilapia nubila was one of the first Lake Victoria cichlids to be exported for the hobby back in the 1970s. Pictured is a male in spawning dress.

scales of other cichlids. The fin- and scale-eating tendencies of this cichlid have not yet been observed in captivity. Provide a varied diet high in protein such as krill, brine shrimp, pellets, and flakes. Supplement the diet with carotene-rich foods to maintain bright coloration.

Breeding: A maternal mouthbrooder. Males establish territories among the rocks, and spawning occurs within the rocks of the male's territory. A brooding female will seek refuge among the rocks. Feed juveniles live baby brine shrimp and finely crushed spirulina flakes.

Name: *Astatotilapia nubila*

Location and Natural Habitat: Found throughout the Lake Victoria basin in lakes, rivers, and swamps. Inhabits shallow, papyrus areas near the shore.

Adult Size: To 4-1/2 inches (11.5 cm).

Husbandry Requirements: A somewhat aggressive species that is best maintained in aquairums no smaller than 75 gallons (280 L). Provide smooth rocks or hardy aquatic plants to serve as territorial markers and places of refuge for those individuals at the bottom of the pecking order. Along with that, a large, sandy area should be established with plenty of space.

Diet: Feeds on aquatic crustaceans and insect larvae in the wild. Provide a varied diet high in protein such as krill, brine shrimp, pellets, and flakes. Supplement the diet with live baby brine shrimp, bloodworms, and mosquito larvae.

Breeding: A maternal mouthbrooder. Males establish territories among the rocks or over the sand near vegetation, and spawning occurs within the male's territory. A brooding female

Astatotilapia piceatus is one of the few species of Astatotilapia that feeds on zooplankton over soft, muddy bottoms. Pictured is a male from the Tanzanian side of Lake Victoria.

will seek refuge among the rocks or vegetation. Feed juveniles live baby brine shrimp and finely crushed spirulina flakes.

Name: *Astatotilapia piceatus*

Location and Natural Habitat: Found in the southern part of the lake in Tanzania from near the shore to at least 60 feet (18 m) deep over muddy substrates.

Adult Size: To 4 inches (10 cm).

Husbandry Requirements: A rather peaceful species that is best maintained in a small school of at least six individuals. Provide plenty of open space, a shallow layer of silica sand, and a few stones scattered about to demarcate territories.

Diet: Feeds on zooplankton found over soft, muddy bottoms. Offer a varied diet of commerically prepared aquarium foods. Supplement the diet with live baby brine shrimp, daphnia, and mosquito larvae.

Breeding: Receptive females will enter the male's territory to spawn. After spawning, the

brooding female may join with the other females to brood her eggs to full term. Feed juveniles live baby brine shrimp and finely crushed flake food.

Name: *Astatotilapia schubotziellus*

Location and Natural Habitat: Found in Lakes Edward and George as well as the Kazinga Channel. Inhabits the shallow, nearshore areas among reed beds.

Adult Size: To 4 inches (10 cm).

Husbandry Requirements: A rather peaceful species that is best maintained in a small school of at least 6 individuals. Provide plenty of open space, a shallow layer of silica sand, and a few stone scattered about to demarcate territories.

Diet: Feeds on aquatic insect larvae and plants in the wild. Offer a varied diet of high-protein foods and commercially prepared foods high in spirulina.

Breeding: Receptive females will enter the male's territory to spawn. After spawning, the brooding female may join with the other

Astatotilapia schubotziellus is found primarily in Lake George and the Kazinga Channel, and, to a lesser extent, within the northern regions of Lake Edward.

Astatotilapia sp. Red Tail is one of the more spectacular species from Lake Victoria that have been collected for the aquarium trade. Pictured is a dominant male.

This female Astatotilapia sp. Red Tail, like nearly all of Lake Victoria's cichlids, exhibits markedly different coloration than males.

females to brood her eggs to full term. Feed juveniles live baby brine shrimp and finely crushed flake food.

Name: *Astatotilapia* sp. Red Tail, Thick Skin, "Haplochromis obliquidens"

Location and Natural Habitat: Found on the east and north coastlines of Lake Victoria. Inhabits shallow, nearshore water.

Adult Size: To 5 inches (12.5 cm).

Husbandry Requirements: An aggressive species that will need a large aquarium of at least 75 gallons (280 L). Provide plenty of rocks piled up to form caves and passageways as well as a thin layer of silica sand. Wild populations are known to dive into the sand to evade danger.

Diet: Consumes aquatic insect larvae in the wild. Offer a varied diet of commercially prepared dried and frozen aquarium fish foods. Supplement the diet with live daphnia and mosquito larvae.

Breeding: A maternal mouthbrooder. Males establish territories among the rocks, and

spawning occurs within the rocks of the male's territory. A brooding female will seek refuge among the rocks. Feed juveniles live baby brine shrimp and finely crushed spirulina flakes.

Name: *Astatotilapia* sp. Spot Bar

Location and Natural Habitat: Captive specimens collected from the Kenyan side of Lake Victoria at Mbita Point. Inhabits the shallow, muddy areas near the shore.

Adult Size: To 5 inches (12.5 cm).

Husbandry Requirements: As an active digger, it should be provided with a shallow layer of silica sand and several smooth stones carefully constructed so as not to become underminded by excessive digging.

Diet: Consumes aquatic insect larvae in the wild. Offer a varied diet of commercially prepared dried and frozen aquarium fish foods. Supplement the diet with live daphnia and mosquito larvae.

Breeding: A maternal mouthbrooder. Males establish territories on the tops of rocks, and spawning occurs within the male's territory.

Astatotilapia sp. Spot Bar is an active digger and should be provided with a shallow layer of fine sand for digging purposes. Pictured is a male in spawning dress.

This female Astatotilapia sp. Spot Bar shows a pattern typical of juveniles and subdominant males.

After spawning, the brooding female may join with the other females to brood her eggs to full term. Feed juveniles live baby brine shrimp and finely crushed flake food.

spawning occurs within the rocks of the male's territory. A brooding female will seek refuge among the rocks. Feed juveniles live baby brine shrimp and finely crushed spirulina flakes.

Name: *Enterochromis erythromaculatus*
Location and Natural Habitat: Originally from Lakes Bulera and Ruhondo and nearby rivers in Rwanda. Has been introduced into Lakes Edward and George. Inhabits the shallow, shoreline area among aquatic grasses and papyrus.
Adult Size: To 4-1/2 inches (11.5 cm).
Husbandry Requirements: A mild-mannered species. Can be maintained in aquariums as small as 30 gallons (110 L). Include some rock work to provide shelter as well as hardy aquatic plants.
Diet: Aquatic insect larvae in the wild. Offer a variety of aquarium foods. Diet should be supplemented with daphnia and mosquito larvae.
Breeding: A maternal mouthbrooder. Males establish territories among the rocks, and

Enterochromis erythromaculatus is one of a few cichlid species that have been artificially introduced into Lake George and Lake Edward. It was originally found in Lake Bulera and Lake Ruhondo and associated rivers in Rwanda. Pictured is a male from Lake George.

Haplochromis limax is one of only a few Lake Victoria basin cichlids that belongs to the genus Haplochromis. Pictured is a male from Lake George.

Name: *Haplochromis limax*

Location and Natural Habitat: Found in Lakes Edward and George as well as the Kazinga Channel. Inhabits the shallow, nearshore areas among reed beds.

Adult Size: To 4 inches (10 cm).

Husbandry Requirements: Best maintained in aquariums no smaller than 50 gallons (190 L). Provide plenty of open space with few rocks, including hardy aquatic plants along with a thin layer of sand.

Diet: Feeds on the algae growing on aquatic plants in the wild. Offer foods high in vegetable matter such as spirulina flakes and algae wafers.

Breeding: A maternal mouthbrooder. Spawning will commence within the male's territory and is likely to occur over the sand near plants or rocks. A brooding female will seek refuge wherever possible. Feed juveniles live baby brine shrimp and finely crushed flake food.

Name: "*Haplochromis*" sp. Big Eye Edward

Location and Natural Habitat: Thus far, found only in the open waters of Lake Edward.

Adult Size: To 4 inches (10 cm).

Husbandry Requirements: Has yet to be collected and imported for the aquarium hobby. Presumably a peaceful, shoaling species not to be maintained with larger, aggressive species.

Diet: Likely feeds on planktonic matter in the water column in the wild.

Breeding: A mouthbrooder, but precise spawning information is lacking since it has not been imported.

Name: "*Haplochromis*" sp. Black Silver Tip

Location and Natural Habitat: Found on the Ugandan side of Lake Victoria. Found in shallow water among the rocks near the shore.

Adult Size: To 5 inches (12.5 cm).

Husbandry Requirements: Best maintained in aquariums no smaller than 50 gallons (190 L).

"Haplochromis" sp. Big Eye Edward is one the of more exciting discoveries made while collecting cichlids at Lake Edward. It was found in the open waters of the lake, and likely represents one of Lake Edward's few planktivores. Pictured is a specimen caught in open water near Katwe Bay.

"Haplochromis" sp. Black Silver Tip was one of several species found and exported back in the mid 1980s from the Ugandan side of Lake Victoria. Pictured is a dominant male.

Provide plenty of rocks piled up to form caves and passageways. Include a thin layer of silica sand. Do not maintain with smaller, less aggressive species.

Diet: Aquatic insect larvae and occasional juvenile cichlids. Offer a varied diet such as pellets, flakes, ocean plankton, frozen foods, and small feeder guppies.

Breeding: A maternal mouthbrooder. Males establish territories among the rocks, and spawning may take place among the rocks or next to the rocks over sand. A brooding female will seek refuge among the rocks. Feed juveniles live baby brine shrimp and finely crushed flake food.

Name: *"Haplochromis"* sp. Blue Bar
Location and Natural Habitat: Found on the eastern shoreline of Lake Victoria at Hippo Point, near Kisumu, Kenya. Inhabits the shallow, muddy, sandy bottoms.
Adult Size: To 4 inches (10 cm).
Husbandry Requirements: Best maintained in aquariums no smaller than 50 gallons (190 L). Provide plenty of rocks piled up to form caves and passageways. Include a thin layer of silica sand. Do not maintain with smaller, less aggressive species.

Diet: Aquatic insect larvae in the wild. Offer a varied diet supplemented with mosquito larvae and daphnia.

Breeding: A maternal mouthbrooder. Males establish territories among the rocks, and spawning may take place among the rocks or next to the rocks over sand. A brooding female will seek refuge among the rocks. Feed juveniles live baby brine shrimp and finely crushed flake food.

Name: *"Haplochromis"* sp. Cherry Fin
Location and Natural Habitat: Found in Lake Nawampasa and possibly Lake Kyoga. Inhabits most biotopes.
Adult Size: To 4 inches (10 cm).
Husbandry Requirements: A relatively peaceful species. Best maintained in aquariums no smaller than 40 gallons (150 L). Provide open sandy areas with few rocks and hardy aquatic plants.

"Haplochromis" sp. Blue Bar is a relatively new import from the Kenyan side of Lake Victoria, at Hippo Point.

"Haplochromis" sp. Cherry Fin was collected from Lake Nawampasa.

Diet: Feeds on aquatic insect larvae in the wild. Offer a varied diet of commercially prepared dried and frozen aquarium fish foods. Supplement the diet with live daphnia and mosquito larvae.

Breeding: A maternal mouthbrooder. The dominant male will establish its territory over sand next to rocks or plants. A brooding female will seek refuge wherever possible. Feed juveniles live baby brine shrimp and finely crushed flake food.

"Haplochromis" sp. Flameback has thus far only been found along the northern shoreline of Lake Victoria. Pictured is a dominant male.

Name: *"Haplochromis"* sp. Flameback
Location and Natural Habitat: Found along the northern shoreline of Lake Victoria. Inhabits areas with an even combination of rocks and sand.
Adult Size: To 5 inches (12.5 cm).
Husbandry Requirements: A somewhat aggressive species, particularly toward its own kind. Best maintained in aquariums no smaller than 50 gallons (190 L). Provide plenty of rocks piled up to form caves and passageways. Include a thin layer of silica sand.
Diet: An insectivore in the wild. Offer a varied diet of commercially prepared dried and frozen aquarium fish foods. Supplement the diet with live daphnia and mosquito larvae.
Breeding: Males establish territories among the rocks, and spawning may take place among the rocks or next to the rocks over sand. A brooding female will seek refuge among the rocks. Feed juveniles live baby brine shrimp and finely crushed flake food.

Name: *"Haplochromis"* sp. Gold Edward (see photo on p. 31).
Location and Natural Habitat: Thus far found only along the shoreline of northern Lake Edward at Katwe Bay. Inhabits the shallow, nearshore areas in less than 3-foot (1 m) deep water.
Adult Size: To 4 inches (10 cm).
Husbandry Requirements: Has yet to be collected and imported for the aquarium hobby. Presumably a moderately aggressive species best maintained with other species of similar size.
Diet: Likely feeds on nearshore aquatic insect larvae found among the reed beds.
Breeding: A mouthbrooder, but precise spawning information is lacking since it has not been imported.

"Haplochromis" sp. Migori Red Chest hails from the Migori River in Kenya. Pictured is a dominant male.

Name: *"Haplochromis"* sp. Migori, Migori Red Chest

Location and Natural Habitat: Found in the Migori River that empties into Lake Victoria in western Kenya.

Adult Size: To 5 inches (12.5 cm).

Husbandry Requirements: A somewhat aggressive species, particularly toward its own kind. Best maintained in aquariums no smaller than 50 gallons (190 L). Provide plenty of rocks piled up to form caves and passageways. Include a thin layer of silica sand.

Diet: Probably an insectivore in the wild. Offer a varied diet of commercially prepared dried and frozen aquarium fish foods. Supplement the diet with live daphnia and mosquito larvae.

Breeding: A maternal mouthbrooder. The dominant male will establish a territory, and spawning will occur within the male's territory. After spawning, the brooding female may join with the other females or retreat to a secluded place to brood her eggs to full term. Feed juveniles live baby brine shrimp and finely crushed flake food.

Name: *"Haplochromis"* sp. Red Edge Edward

Location and Natural Habitat: Thus far found only along the shoreline of northern Lake Edward at Katwe Bay. Inhabits the shallow, nearshore areas in less than 3-foot (1 m) deep water.

Adult Size: To 5 inches (12.5 cm).

Husbandry Requirements: Has yet to be collected and imported for the aquarium hobby. Presumably a moderately aggressive species best maintained with other species of similar size and temperment.

Diet: Likely feeds on nearshore aquatic insect larvae found among the reed beds.

Breeding: A mouthbrooder, but precise spawning information is lacking since it has not been imported.

Name: *"Haplochromis"* sp. Red Piebald

Location and Natural Habitat: Found in the Victoria Nile near Jinja, Lake Nawampasa, and Lake Kyoga. Inhabits most biotopes near the shore.

Adult Size: To 4 inches (10 cm).

"Haplochromis" sp. Red Edge Edward is one of the larger species found within a couple of feet of the shoreline. Its unique head profile makes it easy to tell apart from other Lake Edward species.

"Haplochromis" sp. Red Piebald is an unusual species from the Victorian Nile at Jinja, Lake Kyoga, and Lake Nawampasa in that a majority of specimens collected possess a peibald pattern. Apparently, for males, the normal coloration is a dark blue body, a red anal fin, and red on the outer edge of the dorsal and anal fins. Pictured is a male.

Husbandry Requirements: A relatively peaceful species that should be housed in aquariums no smaller than 50 gallons (190 L). Provide a few hiding places such as smooth stones, hardy aquatic plants, or other smooth structures. Several males and females can be housed together amicably.

"Haplochromis" sp. Ruby is certainly one of the more brilliantly colored species to have been exported from Lake Nawampasa.

Diet: An insectivore in the wild. Offer a varied diet of commercially prepared dried and frozen aquarium fish foods. Supplement the diet with live daphnia and mosquito larvae.

Breeding: A maternal mouthbrooder. Males establish territories among the rocks or reeds, and spawning occurs within the male's territory. A brooding female will seek refuge among the rocks. Feed juveniles live baby brine shrimp and finely crushed spirulina flakes.

Name: *"Haplochromis"* sp. Ruby
Location and Natural Habitat: Found in Lake Nawampasa and Lake Kyoga. Inhabits the plant-filled shoreline of the lake.

Adult Size: To 3-1/2 inches (8.5 cm).

Husbandry Requirements: A relatively peaceful species that should be housed in aquariums no smaller than 50 gallons (190 L). Provide a few hiding places such as smooth stones, hardy aquatic plants, or other smooth structures. Several males and females can be housed together amicably.

Diet: Scrapes algae from aquatic plants in the wild. Offer foods high in vegetable content such as spirulina flakes, dried processed algae sheets, and the like.

Breeding: A maternal mouthbrooder. Males establish territories among the rocks or aquatic plants, and spawning occurs within the male's territory. A brooding female will seek refuge among whatever structures are provided. Feed juveniles live baby brine shrimp and finely crushed spirulina flakes.

Name: *Harpagochromis mentatus*
Location and Natural Habitat: Found in Lake Edward. Inhabits the shallow, nearshore regions over muddy bottoms and papyrus reeds.

*This **Harpagochromis mentatus** was found in extremely shallow water at Katwe Bay, Lake Edward. It likely preys upon the smaller species of cichlids, killifish, and barbs that inhabit this part of the lake.*

Adult Size: To at least 6 inches (15 cm).

Husbandry Requirements: This species has not been imported for the aquarium trade. If and when it does, it would likely need a large aquarium, 100 gallons (375 L), and should not be maintained with any fish small enough to fit into its mouth.

Diet: Consumes small fish in the wild.

Breeding: Unknown, but presumably a maternal mouthbrooder.

Name: *"Harpagochromis"* sp. Blue Rock Hunter

Location and Natural Habitat: Found along the northern and eastern shorelines of Lake Victoria. Probably inhabits the areas where sand and rocks intermingle.

Adult Size: To 5 inches (12.5 cm).

Husbandry Requirements: An aggressive species best maintained in aquariums no smaller than 75 gallons (280 L). Provide plenty of open space and hiding places in the form of rocks piled up to form caves and passageways.

Diet: Piscivorous in the wild. Offer a diet high in protein such as shrimp, krill, and feeder guppies.

Breeding: A maternal mouthbrooder. A dominant male may be particularly hard on unreceptive females. After the spawning act within the male's territory, provide plenty of hiding places for the brooding female to retreat to and away from the aggressive actions of the male. Otherwise, remove the brooding female to a separate aquarium so that she may brood her eggs to full term unmolested. Offer to newly released juveniles live baby brine shrimp and finely crushed flake food.

Name: *"Harpagochromis"* sp. Bronze

Location and Natural Habitat: Thus far found only in offshore waters of northern Lake Edward at Katwe Bay. Likely to inhabit the deeper regions over muddy, rocky bottoms.

Adult Size: To 6 inches (15 cm).

Husbandry Requirements: Has yet to be collected and imported for the aquarium hobby. Presumably a moderately aggressive species best maintained with other species of similar size and temperament.

"Harpagochromis" sp. Blue Rock Hunter was first collected from the northern shoreline of Lake Victoria several years ago. It continues to be a popular species for captive management. Pictured is a male in full spawning dress.

"Harpagochromis" sp. Bronze is one of many undescribed species known to inhabit the deeper waters of Lake Edward. This individual was captured off of Katwe Bay.

Harpagochromis *sp. Pallisa Black Slick is one of the larger predatory species found in Lake Nawampasa and Lake Kyoga. In captivity, however, it ignores other species too large to be swallowed whole.*

Diet: Likely a piscivore in the wild.

Breeding: A mouthbrooder, but precise spawning information is lacking since it has not been imported.

Name: *Harpagochromis* sp. Pallisa Black Slick

Location and Natural Habitat: Found in Lake Nawampasa and probably Lake Kyoga. Inhabits most biotopes.

Adult Size: To 6 inches (15 cm).

Husbandry Requirements: Best maintained in an aquarium no smaller than 75 gallons (280 L). Provide the aquarium with plenty of rocks piled up to form caves and passageways as well as an open sandy area.

Diet: Piscivorous in the wild. Provide a high-protein diet consisting of fresh shrimp, ocean plankton, chopped earthworms, and live feeder guppies.

Breeding: Dominant male will take on a dark brown-green color, similar to the coloration of crude oil. The male will actively court any female that comes within close proximity to his site, which may be on the top

of a rock or at the sand near the rocks. After spawning, the brooding female will leave the male's territory and brood the eggs in seclusion. Feed newly released juveniles live baby brine shrimp and finely crushed flake food.

Name: *"Harpagochromis"* sp. Red Fin Predator

Location and Natural Habitat: Thus far found only in offshore waters of northern Lake Edward at Katwe Bay. Likely to inhabit the deeper regions over muddy, rocky bottoms.

"Harpagochromis" sp. Red Fin Predator is one of the more colorful deepwater species to have been found in Lake Edward. Pictured is a male caught offshore from Katwe Bay.

Adult Size: To 7 inches (17.5 cm).

Husbandry Requirements: Has yet to be collected and imported for the aquarium hobby. Presumably a moderately aggressive species best maintained with other species of similar size and temperment.

Diet: Likely a piscivore in the wild.

Breeding: A mouthbrooder, but precise spawning information is lacking since it has not been imported.

Name: *Harpagochromis* sp. Two Stripe White Lip, *Prognathochromis* sp. All Yellow

Location and Natural Habitat: Was found in the Ugandan side of Lake Victoria. Inhabited relatively shallow water near the shore over sandy, muddy bottoms near rocky areas.

Adult Size: To 7 inches (18 cm).

Husbandry Requirements: A rather mild-mannered species, provided that the aquarium is at least 150 gallons (570 L). Can be somewhat aggressive if maintained in smaller aquariums. Provide plenty of open space with a few large smooth stones or submerged wood as territorial markers.

Diet: Consumes juvenile cichlids in the wild. Offer a variety of high-protein foods. Diet should be supplemented with fresh frozen or live feeder guppies, frozen or freeze-dried ocean plankton, and the like.

Breeding: Vital to maintain domestic stocks of this species since it is extinct in the wild! Dominant male will stake out a territory, usually next to a large rock or submerged tree trunk, and proceed to construct a sand nest. The male maintains an overall dark green-brown coloration, obscuring the horizontal striped pattern seen in the females. A female that is ready to spawn will enter into the male's territory, and spawning will commence within the male's nest. An ovigerous female will leave the male's nest and congregate with other females. Offer to newly released juveniles live baby brine shrimp and finely crushed flake foods.

Name: *"Harpagochromis"* sp. Yellow Snout Predator

Location and Natural Habitat: Thus far found only in offshore waters of northern Lake Edward at Katwe Bay. Likely to inhabit

Harpagochromis *sp. Two Stripe White Lip is one of many species of Lake Victoria cichlids that have become extinct in the lake. This species exists only in captivity. Pictured is a female.*

"Harpagochromis" sp. Yellow Snout Predator is another interesting deepwater species from Lake Edward. Presently, over 100 undescribed species of Haplochromines inhabit Lake Edward!

the deeper regions over muddy, rocky bottoms.

Adult Size: To 7 inches (17.5 cm).

Husbandry Requirements: Has yet to be collected and imported for the aquarium hobby. Presumably a moderately aggressive species best maintained with other species of similar size and temperment.

Diet: Likely a piscivore in the wild.

Breeding: A mouthbrooder, but precise spawning information is lacking since it has not been imported.

Name: *Harpagochromis squamipinnis*

Location and Natural Habitat: Found in Lakes Edward and George as well as in the Kazinga Channel. Juveniles, subadults, and brooding females found near the shore among reed beds, while large adults are found away from shore in deeper water.

Adult Size: To 10 inches (25 cm).

Husbandry Requirements: A large species that will need an aquarium of at least

Harpagochromis squamipinnis *is one of the most abundant species found in Lake George, Lake Edward, and the Kazinga Channel in western Uganda. Pictured is a male starting to develop spawning coloration.*

Hoplotilapia retrodons *commonly occurs in a piebald color variation.*

100-gallon (375 L) capacity. Provide a few large, smooth stones to demarcate territories.

Diet: Piscivorous in the wild. Provide plenty of high-protein foods in captivity such as fresh frozen krill, shrimp, or ocean plankton. Supplement the diet with live feeder guppies or unwanted juvenile cichlids.

Breeding: A maternal mouthbrooder. Dominant males may take on an orange-reddish cast to the body, while females retain an overall silvery color. Spawning will commence within the dominant male's territory. Afterward, the brooding female will retreat to a secluded place to incubate the eggs. Offer to newly released young finely crushed flake food and live baby brine shrimp.

Name: *Hoplotilapia retrodens*

Location and Natural Habitat: Found throughout Lake Victoria. Inhabits the shallow littoral and sublittoral areas over rocky/vegetated areas.

Adult Size: To 7 inches (17.5 cm).

Husbandry Requirements: A mild-mannered species. Best maintained in an aquarium of at least 40 gallons (150 L). Provide ample sandy areas with a few rocks to help demarcate territories.

Labrochromis ishmaeli is another Lake Victoria species that has recently become extinct in the lake. It, too, survives only in captivity. Pictured is a dominant male in spawning dress.

Diet: Consumes snails and some plant material in the wild. Offer a diet of high-protein foods such as chopped clams, ocean plankton, and commercially prepared dry foods. Supplement the diet with foods high in spirulina.

Breeding: Dominant male will stake out a territory and defend it against all other aquarium inhabitants. After the spawning, the brooding female will retreat to a secluded place to incubate her clutch to full term. Provide juveniles with finely crushed flake foods and live baby brine shrimp.

Name: *Labrochromis ishmaeli*
Location and Natural Habitat: Was found in Lake Victoria. The last collected specimens were from the Mwanza Gulf. Inhabited shallow water less than 30 feet (9 m) deep over a soft, organic, muddy bottom.
Adult Size: To 6 inches (15 cm).
Husbandry Requirements: Best maintained in a large, tall aquarium of at least 100-gallon (375 L) capacity. Provide a few large smooth stones to demarcate territories and places for subdominant individuals to retreat to.

Diet: Consumed snails in the wild. Offer a variety of high-protein foods. Supplement the diet with live aquatic snails or fresh frozen clam or mussel flesh.

Breeding: Vital to maintain domestic stocks of this species since it is extinct in the wild! Dominant male will stake out a territory, usually next to a large rock, and proceed to construct a sand nest. The male maintains an overall bright yellow coloration, somewhat obscuring the vertical barring seen in nonsexually active males. A female that is ready to spawn will enter into the male's territory, and spawning will commence within the male's nest. An ovigerous female will leave the male's nest and congregate with other females. Offer to newly released juveniles live baby brine shrimp and finely crushed flake foods.

Name: *Lipochromis* sp. Parvidens-Like
Location and Natural Habitat: Found in Lake Nawampasa and Lake Kyoga. Inhabits most biotopes in both lakes.
Adult Size: To 8 inches (20 cm).

This undescribed Lipochromis species, given the working trade name of Lipochromis sp. Parvidens-like, was collected from Lake Nawampasa. In the wild, it consumes the eggs and larvae of cichlids. Pictured is a male in full spawning dress.

Husbandry Requirements: Aquariums should be at least 100 gallons (375 L). Provide a shallow layer of sand and several large, smooth stones to act as territorial markers. Do not maintain with any other fish small enough to fit into its mouth. Beyond that, relatively mild mannered to fish too large to be considered as food.

Diet: Paedophorous in the wild. Consumes baby fish and embryos by forcibly sucking them from the mouths of brooding female Haplochromines. Offer commercially prepared, high-protein foods. Supplement the diet with feeder guppies.

Breeding: Will require a large aquarium with plenty of open space and a few large smooth stones to demarcate territories and to provide refuge for subdominant males and females. A dominant male will stake out a territory and defend it against all other aquarium inhabitants. If the aquarium is too small, the

Another undescribed Lipochromis *species from Lake Nawampasa is this* Lipochromis *sp. Parvidens shovelmouth. Presently, there are six* Lipochromis *species inhabiting this lake, making it the largest repository of* Lipochromis *species. Pictured is a male in neutral coloration.*

dominant male may kill unreceptive females. After the spawning, the brooding female will retreat to a secluded place to incubate her clutch to full term. Provide juveniles with finely crushed flake foods and live baby brine shrimp.

Name: *Lipochromis* sp. Parvidens Shovelmouth
Location and Natural Habitat: Found in Lake Nawampasa and Lake Kyoga. Inhabits most biotopes in both lakes.

Adult Size: To 7 inches (17.5 cm).

Husbandry Requirements: Aquariums should be at least 100 gallons (375 L). Provide a shallow layer of sand and several large, smooth stones to act as territorial markers. Do not maintain with any other fish small enough to fit into its mouth. Beyond that, relatively mild mannered to fish too large to be considered food.

Diet: Paedophorous in the wild. Consumes baby fish and embryos by forcibly sucking them from the mouths of brooding female Haplochromines. Offer commercially prepared, high-protein foods. Supplement the diet with feeder guppies.

Breeding: Will require a large aquarium with plenty of open space and a few large smooth stones to demarcate territories and provide refuge for subdominant males and females. A dominant male will stake out a territory and defend it against all other aquarium inhabitants. If the aquarium is too small, the dominant male may kill unreceptive females. After the spawning, the brooding female will retreat to a secluded place to incubate her clutch to full term. Provide juveniles with finely crushed flake foods and live baby brine shrimp.

Name: *Macropleurodus bicolor*

Location and Natural Habitat: Once widespread throughout Lake Victoria. Now restricted to Igombe Island within the Speke Gulf of Tanzania. Inhabits sandy and rocky areas in shallow water.

Adult Size: To 7 inches (17.5 cm).

Husbandry Requirements: Will require an aquarium of at least 100 gallons (375 L) for long-term maintenance. Provide plenty of open space with a few large rocks scattered about and a fine layer of silica sand. Dominant males will stake out territories over and between such structures.

Diet: Extracts aquatic snails from their shells as well as aquatic insect larvae in the wild. Offer commercially prepared, high-protein foods. Supplement the diet with chopped clams or mussels.

Breeding: A dominant male will stake out a territory and defend it against all other aquarium inhabitants. After the spawning, the brooding female will retreat to a secluded place to incubate her clutch to full term. Provide juveniles with finely crushed flake foods and live baby brine shrimp.

Name: *Neochromis nigricans*

Location and Natural Habitat: Found along the northern shoreline of Lake Victoria. Inhabits the shallow, inshore areas wherever rocks are present.

Adult Size: To 6 inches (15 cm).

Husbandry Requirements: This large, bulky cichlid will need an aquarium of at least 100 gallons (375 L) for long-term successful captive management. Provide plenty of open space with a few large rocks scattered about and a fine layer of silica sand. Dominant males

This large male Neochromis nigricans *requires ample swimming space and a large aquarium to house it correctly.*

will stake out territories over and between such structures.

Diet: Primarily diatoms in the wild. Offer commercially prepared foods high in algae content such as processed seaweed flakes or spirulina flakes.

Breeding: Will require a large aquarium with plenty of open space and a few large, smooth stones to demarcate territories and for refuge for subdominant males and females. A dominant male will stake out a territory and defend it against all other aquarium inhabitants. After the spawning, the brooding female will retreat to a secluded place to incubate her clutch to full term. Provide juveniles with finely crushed flake foods and live baby brine shrimp.

Name: *Oreochromis esculentus*

Location and Natural Habitat: Found in Lakes Victoria and Kyoga and in some smaller satellite lakes associated with both lakes. Typically inhabits offshore locales over muddy bottoms. Juveniles may be present near the shore in rocky areas. Possibly extinct from Lake Victoria.

The population of this Lake Victoria tilapiine, Oreochromis esculentus, *has been greatly reduced, primarily due to the introduction of the nonnative* Oreochromis niloticus.

Adult Size: To 12 inches (30 cm).

Husbandry Requirements: A large aquarium is required for this robust, heavy eater. The aquarium should be no smaller than 100 gallons (375 L). Provide a shallow layer of sand and a few large, smooth stones to help in demarcating territories.

Diet: Feeds on diatomaceous ooze from the mud in the wild. Offer foods high in vegetable content, such as spirulina flakes and pellets as well as algae wafers.

Breeding: A subtrate spawner. The dominant male will construct a depression in the sand and coax any nearby female to enter the nest to spawn. After a receptive female has entered and spawned, she may leave the male's nest and school with the other females. Offer to newly released juveniles live baby brine shrimp and finely crushed flake food.

Name: *Oreochromis variabilis*
Location and Natural Habitat: Originally from Lake Victoria. Has been introduced throughout most of the Lake Victoria basin.

Adult Size: To 12 inches (30 cm).

Husbandry Requirements: A large aquarium is required for this robust, heavy eater. The aquarium should be no smaller than 100 gallons (375 L). Provide a shallow layer of sand and a few large, smooth stones to help in demarcating territories.

Diet: Phytoplankton and organic matter from the mud in the wild. Offer foods high in vegetable content, such as spirulina flakes and pellets, and algae wafers.

Breeding: A maternal mouthbrooder. The dominant male will construct a depression in the sand and coax any nearby female to enter the nest to spawn. During spawning, the female will take the male's genital tassel into her mouth to gather the sperm to fertilize her eggs. After a receptive female has entered and spawned, she will leave the male's nest and school with the other females. Offer to newly released juveniles live baby brine shrimp and finely crushed flake food.

Name: *Paralabidochromis chilotes*
Location and Natural Habitat: Found only in Lake Victoria. A widespread species occuring

Oreochromis variabilis *is another tilapiine native to Lake Victoria. Notice the unusual genital tassel of this dominant male.*

Paralabidochromis chilotes is found throughout Lake Victoria. This individual was collected from Ugandan waters. Pictured is a subdominant male.

in a multitude of color variants depending on location. Inhabits gently sloping, rocky shorelines. Particularly plentiful where the rocks are quite small.

Adult Size: To 5 inches (12.5 cm).

Husbandry Requirements: A mild-mannered species. Best maintained in an aquarium of at least 40 gallons (150 L). Provide ample sandy areas along with many rocks to form caves and passageways.

Diet: Feeds on aquatic insect larvae living within algae-covered rocks in the wild. Offer foods high in protein such as fresh frozen shrimp, krill, and bloodworms. Supplement the diet with commercially prepared flake and pelleted foods.

Breeding: The dominant male will stake out a territory and defend it against all other aquarium inhabitants. After the spawning, the brooding female will retreat to a secluded place to incubate her clutch to full term. Provide juveniles with finely crushed flake foods and live baby brine shrimp.

Name: *Paralabidochromis labiatus*

Location and Natural Habitat: Found in Lake George, Lake Edward, and the Kazinga Channel. Inhabits the shallow, nearshore areas of both lakes and the channel over muddy bottoms and reed beds.

Adult Size: To 5 inches (12.5 cm).

Husbandry Requirements: Has yet to be collected and imported for the aquarium hobby. Presumably a moderately aggressive species best maintained with other species of similar size and temperment.

Diet: Likely consumes aquatic insect larvae in the wild.

Breeding: A mouthbrooder, but precise spawning information is lacking since it has not been imported.

Name: *Paralabidochromis* sp. Short Head Chilotes

Location and Natural Habitat: Captive specimens originated from the Kenyan side of Lake Victoria at Winam Gulf.

Paralabidochromis labiatus is only one of a couple of Haplochromine species found outside of Lake Victoria proper known to possess thickened lips. Pictured is a subadult caught in shallow water at Katwe Bay, Lake Edward.

A similar looking species to P. chilotes, this Paralabidochromis sp. Short Head Chilotes was collected in Kenyan waters, in Winam Gulf. This undescribed species is also found in Tanzanian waters. Pictured is a male.

Adult Size: To 5 inches (12.5 cm).

Husbandry Requirements: A mild-mannered species. Best maintained in an aquarium of at least 40 gallons (150 L). Provide ample sandy areas along with many rocks to form caves and passageways.

Diet: Feeds on aquatic insect larvae living within algae-covered rocks in the wild. Offer foods high in protein such as fresh frozen shrimp, krill, and bloodworms. Supplement the diet with commercially prepared flake and pelleted foods.

Breeding: The dominant male will stake out a territory and defend it against all other aquarium inhabitants. After the spawning, the brooding female will retreat to a secluded place to incubate her clutch to full term. Provide juveniles with finely crushed flake foods and live baby brine shrimp.

Name: *Paralabidochromis paucidens*

Location and Natural Habitat: Found only in Lake Kivu. Inhabits the shallow, rocky shoreline of the lake.

Paralabidochromis paucidens *is native to Lake Kivu and is known to occur in several color variations. This male is considered a blue variant.*

Pictured is a male of the yellow color variant of **Paralabidochromis paucidens.**

Adult Size: To 4 inches (10 cm).

Husbandry Requirements: Should be provided with an aquarium of at least 50 gallons (190 L). Offer some open space and several rocks piled up to form caves and passageways.

Diet: Aquatic insect larvae in the wild. Offer a variety of commercially prepared aquarium foods. Supplement diet with mosquito larvae and daphnia.

Breeding: A maternal mouthbrooder. A dominant male may spawn over or within the rocks of his territory. After spawning, the brooding female will retreat to a secluded place to brood her eggs to full term. Offer to newly released juveniles live baby brine shrimp and finely crushed flake food.

Name: *Prognathochromis perrieri,* Haplochromis pellegrini

Location and Natural Habitat: Originally collected from the Ugandan side of Lake Victoria. Roamed over areas where the sand and rocks intermingled.

Adult Size: To 5-1/2 inches (14 cm).

Husbandry Requirements: Best maintained in an aquarium no smaller than 75 gallons (280 L). Provide the aquarium with plenty of rocks piled up to form caves and passageways as well as an open, sandy area.

Diet: Piscivorous in the wild. Provide a high-protein diet consisting of fresh shrimp, ocean plankton, chopped earthworms, and live feeder guppies.

Breeding: Vital to maintain domestic stocks of this species since it is extinct in the wild! A dominant male will stake out a territory, usually next to a large rock, and proceed to

Prognathochromis sp. Dentex-like is a small, cryptic ambush predator from Lake Nawampasa and Lake Kyoga.

construct a sand nest. A female that is ready to spawn will enter into the male's territory, and spawning will commence within the male's nest. The ovigerous female will leave the male's nest and find a secluded place to brood her eggs. Offer to newly released juveniles live baby brine shrimp and finely crushed flake foods.

Name: *Prognathochromis* sp. Dentex-Like

Location and Natural Habitat: Found in Lake Nawampasa and possibly Lake Kyoga. Inhabits most biotopes in search of prey.

Adult Size: To 5 inches (12.5 cm).

Husbandry Requirements: A rather cryptic species that can be maintained in aquariums as small as 50 gallons (190 L). Provide plenty of rocks piled up to form caves and passageways in order to make this species feel secure. Do not maintain with any fish small enough to be swallowed by this species.

Diet: A persuit piscivore in the wild. Offer commercially prepared, high-protein foods such as fresh shrimp and krill. Supplement the diet with feeder guppies.

Prognathochromis perrieri is considered to be extinct in Lake Victoria. As such, it is vitally important to maintain captive spawning populations of this species. Pictured is a male.

Breeding: A maternal mouthbrooder. A dominant male may spawn over the sand near a loosely defined territory. After spawning, the brooding female will retreat to a secluded place to brood her eggs to full term. Offer to newly released juveniles live baby brine shrimp and finely crushed flake food.

Name: *Prognathochromis cf. worthingtoni*, Big Red, Torpedo Kribensis

Location and Natural Habitat: Found in Lake Nawampasa and Lake Kyoga. Inhabits most biotopes in search of prey.

Adult Size: To 8 inches (20 cm).

Husbandry Requirements: A moderately peaceful predator that should be maintained in an aquarium of at least 100 gallons (375 L). Provide plenty of open space with a fine layer of silica sand and a few large, smooth stones

Prognathochromis cf. worthingtoni, *known as Torpedo Kribensis, is another cryptic ambush predator from Lake Nawampasa and Lake Kyoga. The splash of red on the breast and cheek give this species a more attractive appearance than many* **Prognathochromis** *species.*

Psammochromis graueri *is one of the more commonly encountered species found along the rocky shorelines of Lake Kivu. Pictured is a male.*

to help demarcate territories and to provide some security. Do not maintain with any fish small enough to be swallowed by this species.

Diet: Piscivorous in the wild. Offer commercially prepared, high-protein foods such as fresh shrimp and krill. Supplement the diet with feeder guppies.

Breeding: A maternal mouthbrooder. A dominant male may spawn over the sand near a loosely defined territory. After spawning, the brooding female will retreat to a secluded place to brood her eggs to full term. Offer to newly released juveniles live baby brine shrimp and finely crushed flake food.

Name: *Psammochromis graurei*

Location and Natural Habitat: Found only in Lake Kivu. Inhabits the shallow, rocky shoreline of the lake. Most active in the early morning and late evening.

Adult Size: To 4-1/2 inches (11.5 cm).

Husbandry Requirements: Should be provided an aquarium of at least 50 gallons

(190 L). Offer some open space and several rocks piled up to form caves and passageways.

Diet: Aquatic insect larvae in the wild. Offer a variety of commercially prepared aquarium foods. Supplement diet with mosquito larvae and daphnia.

Breeding: A maternal mouthbrooder. A dominant male may spawn over or within the rocks of his territory. After spawning, the brooding female will retreat to a secluded place to brood her eggs to full term. Offer to newly released juveniles live baby brine shrimp and finely crushed flake food.

Name: *Ptyochromis* sp. Hippo Point Salmon
Location and Natural Habitat: Found on the eastern shoreline of Lake Victoria at Hippo Point, near Kisumu, Kenya. Inhabits the shallow, muddy, sandy bottoms.

Adult Size: To 5-1/2 inches (14 cm).

Husbandry Requirements: A moderately sized species that will need an aquarium of at least 75-gallon (280 L) capacity. Provide some rock work to serve as shelter and to demarcate territories while giving ample open space since this species prefers to deport out in the open.

Diet: An oral sheller in the wild. It specializes in extracting aquatic snails from their shells without crushing the shell in the process. Offer high-protein foods supplementing the diet with live, freshwater snails, fresh frozen chopped clams, or mussels.

Breeding: A maternal mouthbrooder. Males establish territories near the rocks, and spawning occurs over sand within the male's territory. A brooding female may seek refuge among the rocks. If the aquarium is large enough, the brooding female may join with the other females in the open. Feed juveniles

This attractive Lake Victoria native, Ptyochromis sp. Hippo Point Salmon, was originally collected from Hippo Point, an area near Kisumu, Kenya. Pictured is a male in spawning dress.

live baby brine shrimp and finely crushed spirulina flakes.

Name: *Ptyochromis xenognathus*
Location and Natural Habitat: Found throughout Lake Victoria. Captive specimens originated from Tanzanian waters. Typically inhabits the shallow, sandy areas near the shore. Male color pattern tends to be blue in sand-dwelling populations, while those that occasionally frequent rocky areas have a greenish coloration in the male sex.

Adult Size: To 5 inches (12.5 cm).

Husbandry Requirements: A moderately peaceful species. The aquarium should be no smaller than 50 gallons (190 L). Provide a few rocks and plenty of open space over a shallow layer of silica sand. Best to maintain at least six together.

Diet: Extracts snails from their shells in the wild. Offer a varied, high-protein diet such as fresh shrimp, chopped clams, mussels, and

Ptyochromis xenognathus has been known to dive into the sand when threatened. This defense mechanism is unique to this Lake Victoria cichlid. Pictured is a male.

Female Pundamilia nyererei from most known geographic locations in Lake Victoria sport an identical color pattern. For this reason, differing color variants of P. nyererei should not be maintained together in the same aquarium. Pictured is a female from Ruti Island, Tanzania.

ocean plankton. Supplement the diet with live aquatic snails.

Breeding: A maternal mouthbrooder. Males establish territories near the rocks, and spawning occurs over sand within the male's territory. A brooding female may seek refuge among the rocks. If the aquarium is large enough, the brooding female may join with the other females in the open. Feed juveniles live baby brine shrimp and finely crushed spirulina flakes.

Name: *Pundamilia nyererei*
Location and Natural Habitat: Found along the southeast shoreline in Tanzania as well as at the eastern shoreline in Kenya. Inhabits shallow, rocky areas.
Adult Size: To 4 inches (10 cm).
Husbandry Requirements: Should be maintained in groups of six to ten. A moderately aggressive species. Will need an aquarium no smaller than 50 gallons (190 L) with plenty of rocks piled up to form caves and passageways. The dominant male will actively

Pundamilia nyererei *is perhaps the most celebrated species to have come out of Lake Victoria in several years. It appears to be common in the south and eastern shorelines of the lake. Pictured is a male from Ruti Island, Tanzania.*

chase subdominant males and unreceptive females.

Diet: Algae, zooplankton, and phytoplankton in the wild. Offer a variety of aquarium foods. Diet should be supplemented with spirulina flakes and live baby brine shrimp.

Pundamilia sp. Crimson Tide is closely related to P. nyererei, but lacks the brilliant coloration. Pictured is a male from the Ugandan side of Lake Victoria.

Breeding: A maternal mouthbrooder. Males establish territories among the rocks, and spawning occurs within the rocks of the male's territory. A brooding female will seek refuge among the rocks. Feed juveniles live baby brine shrimp and finely crushed spirulina flakes.

Name: *Pundamilia* sp. Crimson Tide
Location and Natural Habitat: Found in the north and northeastern area of Lake Victoria within Uganda and Kenya, respectively. Inhabits shallow, rocky areas.
Adult Size: To 4 inches (10 cm).
Husbandry Requirements: An aggressive species that should be maintained in an aquarium no smaller than 50 gallons (190 L) with plenty of rocks piled up to form caves and passageways. Best kept in a group of at least six individuals. The dominant male will actively

chase subdominant males and unreceptive females.
Diet: Algae and plankton in the wild. Offer a variety of aquarium foods. Diet should be supplemented with spirulina flakes and live baby brine shrimp.
Breeding: A maternal mouthbrooder. Males establish territories among the rocks, and spawning occurs within the rocks of the male's territory. A brooding female will seek refuge among the rocks. Feed juveniles live baby brine shrimp and finely crushed spirulina flakes.

Name: *Pundamilia* sp. Rock Kribensis
Location and Natural Habitat: Found throughout Lake Victoria wherever rocky environs are present.
Adult Size: To 5 inches (12.5 cm).
Husbandry Requirements: An aggressive species that should be maintained in an aquarium no smaller than 50 gallons (190 L) with plenty of rocks piled up to form caves and passageways. Best kept in a group of at least six individuals. The dominant male will actively

Pundamilia sp. Rock Kribensis was one of several new species that were exported from Lake Victoria back in the mid 1980s. This attractive species has generated a strong following among hobbyists worldwide. Pictured is a large male from Uganda.

Pundamilia sp. Rock Kribensis is found throughout much of Lake Victoria, wherever rock environs are present. This Kenyan color variant has more yellow on its flank than does the variant from Uganda.

chase subdominant males and unreceptive females.

Diet: Algae and plankton in the wild. Offer a variety of aquarium foods. Diet should be supplemented with spirulina flakes and live baby brine shrimp.

Breeding: A maternal mouthbrooder. Males establish territories among the rocks, and spawning occurs within the rocks of the male's territory. A brooding female will seek refuge among the rocks. Feed juveniles live baby brine shrimp and finely crushed spirulina flakes.

Name: *Pyxichromis orthostoma*
Location and Natural Habitat: Lake Kyoga and Lake Nawampasa. Roams freely through the plants and open, sandy areas.
Adult Size: To 8 inches (20 cm).
Husbandry Requirements: Best maintained in a large, tall aquarium of at least 100-gallon (375 L) capacity. Provide a few large, smooth stones to demarcate territories and places for subdominant individuals to retreat to.
Diet: An ambush predator in the wild. Offer a variety of high-protein foods in captivity. Supplement the diet with live feeder guppies or unwanted juvenile cichlids.
Breeding: Moderately aggressive during courtship and spawning. Provide plenty of

This young, sexually active male **Pundamilia** *sp. Rock Kribensis from Ugandan waters shows a more well-defined pattern than do larger, older males.*

In spite of its cavernous mouth, **Pyxichromis** **orthostoma** *is peaceful toward any other fish too large to be engulfed in its impressive maw.*

space for the dominant male to stake out a territory as well as enough refuge for brooding and nonbrooding females to retreat to if overly harassed by the male. Offer to newly released

Pyxichromis *sp. Gold Large Mouth is one of several piscivorous species found in Lake Nawampasa and Lake Kyoga. It is a peaceful species toward those fish too large to be swallowed whole.*

juveniles live baby brine shrimp and finely crushed flake foods.

Name: *Pyxichromis* sp. Gold Large Mouth
Location and Natural Habitat: Found in Lake Nawampasa and Lake Kyoga. Inhabits a variety of substrata in search of prey items.

Adult Size: To 5 inches (12.5 cm).

Husbandry Requirements: A mild-mannered species that can be maintained in aquariums as small as 50 gallons (190 L). Provide a varied biotope with open space, a fine layer of silica sand, and several rocks piled up to form caves and passageways.

Diet: Feeds on small fish in the wild. Offer a variety of high-protein foods in captivity. Supplement the diet with live feeder guppies.

Breeding: A maternal mouthbrooder. Spawning takes place within the male's territory. A brooding female will seek refuge among whatever structures are provided in the aquarium. Feed juveniles live baby brine shrimp and finely crushed flake food.

Name: *Thoracochromis petronius*

Location and Natural Habitat: Found primarily in Kashaka Bay, Lake George. Inhabits shallow, rocky areas along the perimeter of this extinct volcanic bay.

Adult Size: To 4-1/2 inches (11.5 cm).

Husbandry Requirements: Unkown. Not yet imported for the aquarium trade. If imported, an aquarium of at least 50 gallons (190 L) with plenty of rocks piled up to form caves and passageways would be appropriate.

Diet: Aquatic insects and their larvae in the wild. Offer a variety of commercially prepared aquarium foods. Diet should be supplemented with spirulina flakes and live baby brine shrimp.

Breeding: Unkown, but likely a maternal mouthbrooder. Thus far, only males have been captured. Females have yet to be found.

Name: *Tridontochromis* sp. Silver Stilleto, Longsnout

Location and Natural Habitat: Found in Lake Nawampasa and Lake Kyoga. Inhabits a variety of biotopes.

Adult Size: To 4-1/2 inches (11.5 cm).

Thoracochromis petronius *is native to Lake George, and is found primarily in Kashaka Bay, where the shoreline is steeply sloping and rocky.*

Tridontochromis *sp. Silver Stilleto from Lake Nawampasa and Lake Kyoga is the only remaining species of the genus* **Tridontochromis** *known to exist in the Lake Victoria basin.*

Husbandry Requirements: A mild-mannered species that can be maintained in aquariums as small as 40 gallons (150 L). Provide a varied biotope with open space, a fine layer of silica sand, and several rocks piled up to form caves and passageways.

Diet: Primarily juvenile cichlids and aquatic crustaceans. Offer a variety of high-protein foods in captivity. Supplement the diet with live feeder guppies and ghost shrimp.

Breeding: A maternal mouthbrooder. Spawning will take place within the male's territory. A brooding female will seek refuge among whatever structures are provided in the aquarium. Feed juveniles live baby brine shrimp and finely crushed flake food.

Name: *Xystichromis phytophagus*

Location and Natural Habitat: Found in Lake Kanyaboli in western Kenya. Inhabits the plant-infested, muddy bottoms near the shore.

Adult Size: To 4-1/2 inches (11.5 cm).

Husbandry Requirements: A moderately aggressive species that should be maintained

Xystichromis phytophagus appears to be native to Lake Kanyaboli, just east of Lake Victoria, in western Kenya. It is one of only a handful of Lake Victoria basin Haplochromines that consumes plant matter as a principal component of its diet. Pictured is a male.

in aquariums of at least 50 gallons (190 L). Provide a few smooth stones, aquatic plants, and plenty of open space with a sandy bottom.

Diet: Feeds on aquatic plants in the wild. Will consume a wide variety of commercially prepared aquarium foods. Supplement the diet with spirulina flake food and algae wafers.

Breeding: A maternal mouthbrooder. The dominant male will construct a shallow depression in the sand as his spawning site and coax any receptive female into the depression to spawn. Once spawning is completed, the female will retreat to a secluded area to brood her eggs to full term. Feed juveniles live baby brine shrimp and finely crushed flake food.

Name: *Xystichromis* sp. Dayglow Fulu
Location and Natural Habitat: Found in Lake Kanyaboli in western Kenya. Inhabits the plant-infested, muddy bottoms near the shore.
Adult Size: To 4-1/2 inches (11.5 cm).

Husbandry Requirements: An aggressive species, best maintained in an aquarium of at least 75 gallons (280 L). Provide plenty of open space with a sandy bottom. A few smooth stones and aquatic plants may be added to help demarcate territories and to make them feel more secure.

Diet: Feeds on aquatic invertebrates in the wild. Offer a variety of commercially prepared aquarium foods. Diet should be supplemented with mosquito larvae and daphnia.

Breeding: A maternal mouthbrooder. The dominant male will construct a shallow depression in the sand as his spawning site and coax any receptive female into the depression to spawn. Once spawning is completed, the female will retreat to a secluded area to brood her eggs to full term. Feed juveniles live baby brine shrimp and finely crushed flake food.

Name: *Xystichromis* sp. All Red, Kyoga Flameback
Location and Natural Habitat: Found in Lake Kyoga and Lake Nawampasa. Lives among the aquatic plants surrounding the perimeter of the lake.

Xystichromis sp. Dayglow Fulu is another Lake Kanyaboli native.

Xystichromis sp. All Red from Lake Nawampasa and Lake Kyoga probably has more red coloration on its body than any other Lake Victoria basin Haplochromine.

Adult Size: To 4 inches (10 cm).

Husbandry Requirements: A mild-mannered species. Best maintained in an aquarium of at least 40 gallons (150 L). Provide ample sandy areas with aquatic plants and some smooth stones to help demarcate territories.

Diet: Consumes plants in the wild. Offer foods high in vegetable content such as spirulina flakes and algae wafers.

Breeding: A maternal mouthbrooder. The dominant male will construct a shallow

Yissochromis laparogramma is one of the more critically endangered species of the genus Yissochromis. Pictured is a male captured offshore from Kiumba Beach, Kenya, Lake Victoria.

depression in the sand as his spawning site and coax any receptive female into the depression to spawn. Once spawning is completed, the female will retreat to a secluded area to brood her eggs to full term. Feed juveniles live baby brine shrimp and finely crushed spirulina flake food.

Name: *Yissochromis laparogramma*

Location and Natural Habitat: Found in the open waters of Lake Victoria. More common in the eastern half of the lake.

Adult Size: To 4 inches (10 cm).

Husbandry Requirements: A rather peaceful, gregarious species. Best to maintain several together in an aquarium no smaller than 40 gallons (150 L). Provide a shallow layer of silica sand on the bottom and no rocks. Lighting should be subdued.

Diet: A zooplanktivore in the wild. Offer a varied diet of live and frozen brine shrimp, flakes, small pellets, and ocean plantkon. Supplement the diet with small live foods such as daphnia, live baby brine shrimp, mosquito larvae, and the like.

Breeding: An open-water spawner. Provide an open aquarium with very few rocks and a shallow layer of silica sand. Feed juveniles live baby brine shrimp and finely crushed spirulina flakes.

Name: *Yissochromis pyrrocephalus*

Location and Natural Habitat: Found in the open waters of Lake Victoria. More common in the southern half of the lake.

Adult Size: To 4 inches (10 cm).

Husbandry Requirements: A rather peaceful, gregarious species. Best to maintain several together in an aquarium no smaller than

The pelagic planktivore Yissochromis
pyrrocephalus *from Lake Victoria was at
one point critically endangered. Thanks to
overfishing of the Nile perch, this small and
peaceful cichlid is now quite common in the
lake. Pictured in the foreground is a
subdominant male.*

40 gallons (150 L). Provide a shallow layer of
silica sand on the bottom and no rocks. Lighting should be subdued.

Diet: A zooplanktivore in the wild. Offer a
varied diet of live and frozen brine shrimp,
flakes, small pellets, and ocean plantkon. Supplement the diet with small live foods such as
daphnia, live baby brine shrimp, mosquito larvae, and the like.

Breeding: An open-water spawner. Provide
an open aquarium with very few rocks and a
shallow layer of silica sand. Feed juveniles live
baby brine shrimp and finely crushed spirulina
flakes.

Name: *Yissochromis* sp. Argens
Location and Natural Habitat: Found in
Lake Victoria. Captive specimens originated

from Tanzanian waters. Inhabits the open
waters near the surface.

Adult Size: To 4 inches (10 cm).

Husbandry Requirements: A rather peaceful, gregarious species. Best to maintain several
together in an aquarium no smaller than 40
gallons (150 L). Provide a shallow layer of silica
sand on the bottom and no rocks. Lighting
should be subdued.

Diet: A zooplanktivore in the wild. Offer a
varied diet of commercially prepared aquarium
foods. Supplement the diet with live baby
brine shrimp, daphnia, and mosquito larvae.

Breeding: An open-water spawner. Provide an
open aquarium with very few rocks and a shallow layer of silica sand. Feed juveniles live baby
brine shrimp and finely crushed spirulina flakes.

Yissochromis *sp. Argens is another pelagic
zooplanktivorous species native to Lake
Victoria. This species tends to be found more
along the surface in open waters than other*
Yissochromis *species. Pictured is a male in
spawning dress.*

Clockwise on p. 88 from top left:
"Haplochromis" *sp. Black Silver Tip male;* Ptyochromis *sp. Hippo Point Salmon male;* Astatotilapia latifasciata *male;* Astatotilapia *sp. Spot Bar male;* Yissochromis pyrrocephalus *male;* Astatotilapia *sp. Red Tail male. Clockwise on p. 89 from top left:* Astatotilapia macropsoides; Lipochromis *sp. Parvidens-like female;* "Haplochromis" *sp. Red Piebald male;* Xystichromis phytophagus *male;* Harpugochromis squamipinnis *juvenile;* Prognathochromis perrieri *male.*

GLOSSARY

Anoxic: totally devoid of oxygen

Biotope: a living organism's natural habitat

Carnivore: a flesh-eating animal

Conspecific: term applied to individuals of the same species

Cryptic: camouflage; an animal with a color pattern that mimics the color or shape of its habitat

Ctenoid scale: circular scale with several small, pointed projections on its outer edge

Cycloid scale: circular scale with smooth edges all around

Detritivore, detritivorous: an animal that eats organic waste

Genital tassel: a fleshy, branchlike structure located just behind the anus on certain male Tilapiine cichlids; this structure becomes particularly enlarged during periods of sexual activity

Hectare: an area of 10,000 square meters or 2,471 acres

Herbivorous: a plant-eating animal

Heterotrophic bacteria: bacteria capable of using various organic materials for their food and energy needs

Hybridization: two distinct species inter-breeding and producing offspring with the combined genetic makeup of the two species

kH: carbonate hardness; the measurement of the amount of carbonate, or bicarbonate, in water

Lateral line: a series of receptors embedded in the scales of a fish that can usually be seen as a narrow line running horizontally down the body; these receptors enable the fish to detect nearby movement in the water

Mollusks: shelled invertebrates, such as snails and clams

Monophyletic: a group of related organisms derived from a common ancestor

Paedophore, paedophorous: an animal that eats the eggs, embryos, or young of another animal

Pelagic: living in the open water away from the shoreline

pH: a value on a scale of 0 to 14 that indicates the acidity or alkalinity of water; acidic water has a pH less than 7, and alkaline water has a pH higher than 7

Pharyngeal bone: bones located in the throat and studded with teeth that aid in the mastication of food

Phytoplankton: microscopic plants, usually algae, that float in the water

Piscivore, piscivorous: an animal that eats fish

Planktivore, planktivorous: an animal that eats free-floating phytoplankton and zoo-plankton

Polyphyletic: a group of related organisms derived from several distinct ancestors

Zooplankton: tiny aquatic animals, usually crustaceans and insect larvae, that float in the water

*This is a fine example of a male **Astatotilapia aeneocolor**. (See description on p. 57.)*

INFORMATION

Magazines

Tropical Fish Hobbyist
TFH Publications, Inc.
211 West Sylvania Avenue
Neptune, NJ 07753
908-988-8400

Aquarium Fish Magazine
Fancy Publications, Inc.
Subscription Department
P.O. Box 53351
Boulder, CO 80323-3351

Cichlid News Magazine
Aquatic Promotions, Inc.
P.O. Box 522842
Miami, FL 33152
305-593-0088

Journals

Ichthyological Explorations of Fresh Waters
Verlag Dr. Friedrich Pfiel
P.O. Box 65 00 86
D-81214, München, Germany

Books

Konings, Ad. *Enjoying Cichlids*. St. Leon-Rot,
    Germany: Cichlid Press, 1993.
_____. *Back to Nature Guide to Malawi
    Cichlids*. Jonsered, Sweden: Fohrman
    Aquaristik AB, 1997.
Loiselle, Dr. Paul. *The Cichlid Aquarium*.
    Blacksburg, Virginia: Tetra Press, 1994.
Seehausen, Ole. *Lake Victoria Rock Cichlids*.
    Gottingen, Germany: Verduijn Cichlids, 1996.

Book Dealers

Aquatic Book Shop
P.O. Box 2150
Shingle Springs, CA 95682-2150
530-622-7157

Cichlid Press
4170 Valplano Drive
El Paso, TX 79912

Aquatic Promotions, Inc.
P.O. Box 522842
Miami, FL 33152
Tel/Fax: 305-593-0088

Finley Aquatic Books
150 North Road
Pascoag, RI 02859
Tel: 401 568-0371
Fax: 401 568-1561

National Cichlid Clubs

American Cichlid Association
130 Springbrook Lane
Stockbridge, GA 30281

Pacific Coast Cichlid Association
P.O. Box 28145
San Jose, CA 95128

Greater Chicago Cichlid Association
41 West 510 Route 20
Hampshire, IL 60140

International Cichlid Clubs
Germany
Deutsche Cichliden Gesellschaft
Parkstrasse 21a
D-33719 Bielfeld

England
British Cichlid Association
248 Longridge, Knutsford
Cheshire, WA18 8PH

France
Association France Cichlid
15 Rue des Hirondelles
f-67350 Daunendorf

Netherlands
Nederlandse Cichliden Vereniging
Boeier 31
NL-1625 CJ Hoorn

Internet Sites
Aquatic Book Shop
http://www.seahorses.com

Cichlid Press
http://www.cichlidpress.com

The Cichlid Room Companion
http://www.petsforum.com/cichlidroom/default.html

Astatotilapia sp. "Spot Bar" male in the act of yawning.

A young male Paralabidochromis chilotes.

Safety Around the Aquarium
 Water and electricity can lead to dangerous accidents. Therefore, you should make absolutely sure when buying equipment that it is suitable for use in an aquarium.
✔ Every technical device must have the UL sticker on it. These letters give the assurance that the safety of the equipment has been carefully checked by experts and that "with ordinary use" (as the experts say) nothing dangerous can happen.
✔ Always unplug any electrical equipment before you do any cleaning around or in the aquarium.
✔ Never do your own repairs on the aquarium or the equipment if there is something wrong with it. As a matter of safety, all repairs should only be carried out by an expert.

INDEX

Important Notes

Electrical equipment for aquarium care is described in this book. Please do not fail to read the note on p. 92, since otherwise serious accidents could occur.

Water damage from broken glass, overflowing, or tank leaks cannot always be avoided. Therefore, you should not fail to take out insurance.

Please take special care that neither children nor adults ever eat any aquarium plants. It can cause serious health injury. Fish medication should be kept away from children.

Dedication

To my grandmother, Charlotte Duhn, who has always shown herself to be a true prayer warrior.

Acknowledgments

The author wishes to thank the following people who, over the years, offered their unyielding hospitality and access to their ideas, theories, or fish to photograph. Many have given of their time to help me understand various perplexing concepts and ideas. My deepest apologies if I have inadvertently omitted those who figured significantly in my evolving knowledge of the cichlids of the Lake Victoria basin.

I would also like to thank the following people for their mutual interests in the cichlids of the Lake Victoria basin and for offering up their ideas as well as those who have graciously given me access to their cichlids for photographing purposes: Rich Becktell, Rich and Laura Birley, Dr. Warren Burgess, Justine Cavanagh, Mark Chandler of the New England Aquarium and also for his invaluable help in identifying the species photographed at the aquarium and for various ideas discussed and questions asked, Ron Coleman, Phil Farrel, Lee Finley, Jim and Agnes Forshey, Tim Hovanec, Ray Hunziker, Ad Konings, Dan Laughlin, Dr. Paul Loiselle, John Lombardo, Oliver Lucanus, Steve Lundblad, Kaana Mbaga of the Uganda Fisheries Department at Kesese, John Niemans, Art North, Ralph Paccione, Chuck Rambo, Amy Rodgers, Robert Rodriquez, Ben Rosler, Delores Schehr, Ron Sousy, Steve Spina for showing me around the New England Aquarium and for his patience with my many questions, Dick Strever, and Jerry Walls.

Cover Photos

Mark Phillip Smith

Photo Credits

Ad Konings: pages 6, 12 (left), 15 (bottom left and right), 39 (top right), 58, 70 (right), 76 (top right and bottom), 78 (right); Oliver Lucanus: pages 15 (top right), 85 (bottom); all other photos by Mark Phillip Smith.

About the Author

Mark Phillip Smith is a professional wildlife photographer, explorer, and discoverer of freshwater temperate and tropical fishes. In 1990, he contributed to the discovery of a genus and two species of Lake Malawi Cichlids. In 1994, he discovered several new species of cichlids in Lake Edward, Uganda. His ichthyological interests have taken him to Japan, Mexico, Uruguay, Malawi, Zambia, Zimbabwe, Kenya, Uganda, England, Sweden, Hawaii, and the Caribbean. He writes for domestic and international publications, and lectures on cichlids and other tropical fish.

© Copyright 2001 by Mark Phillip Smith

All rights reserved.
No part of this book may be reproduced in any form, by photostat, microfilm, xerography, or any other means, or incorporated into any information retrieval system, electronic or mechanical, without the written permission of the copyright owner.

All inquiries should be addressed to:
Barron's Educational Series, Inc.
250 Wireless Boulevard
Hauppauge, NY 11788
http://www.barronseduc.com

International Standard Book No. 0-7641-1811-0

Library of Congress Catalog Card No. 2001025042

Library of Congress Cataloging-in-Publication Data
Smith, Mark Phillip, 1966-
    Lake Victoria basin cichlids : everything about history, setting up an aquarium, health concerns, and spawning / Mark Phillip Smith.
        p. cm. — (Complete pet owner's manual)
    ISBN 0-7641-1811-0 (alk. paper)
        1. Cichlids—Victoria, Lake, Watershed.
    2. Aquarium fishes. I. Title. II. Series.

SF458.C5 S55 2001
639.3'774—dc21   2001025042

Printed in Hong Kong
9 8 7 6 5 4 3 2 1